**CHET BUSH**

THE STORY *of*

DR. CHARLES JOHNSON

# CALLED *TO* THE FIRE

A WITNESS *for* GOD IN MISSISSIPPI

D0005399

ABINGDON PRESS

*Nashville*

# CALLED *TO* THE FIRE

*This book is printed on acid-free paper.*

**Library of Congress Cataloging-in-Publication Data**

Bush, Chet.
    Called to the fire : a witness for God in Mississippi : the story of Dr. Charles Johnson / Chet Bush.
       p.  cm.
    ISBN 978-1-4267-5328-2 (hardback : alk. paper)  1. Johnson, Charles, 1938 March 5-  2. African Americans—Civil rights—Mississippi—History—20th century.  3. African American clergy—Biography.  4. Civil rights workers—Mississippi—Biography.  5. Church of the Nazarene—United States—Clergy—Biography.  6. Trials (Murder)—Mississippi—Meridian.  7. Murder—Mississippi—Neshoba County—History—20th century.  8. Civil rights workers—Crimes against—Mississippi—Neshoba County—History—20th century.  9. Mississippi—Race relations—History—20th century.  I. Title.
    E185.93.M6B88 2012
    323.092—dc23
[B}

                                                                    2012038104

All scripture quotations, unless noted otherwise, are taken from the *New Revised Standard Version of the Bible,* copyright 1989, Division of Christian Education of the National Council of the Churches of Christ in the United States of America. Used by permission. All rights reserved.

Scripture quotations marked KJV are from the King James or Authorized Version of the Bible.

Quotations from Martin Luther King Jr. are reprinted by arrangement with The Heirs to the Estate of Martin Luther King Jr., c/o Writers House as agent for the proprietor New York, NY. Copyright 1963 Dr. Martin Luther King Jr.; copyright renewed 1991 Coretta Scott King.

Photo Credits: personal photos used with permission from Chet Bush, Becky Combs, and Charles Johnson.

12 13 14 15 16 17 18 19 20 21—10 9 8 7 6 5 4 3 2 1
MANUFACTURED IN THE UNITED STATES OF AMERICA

# CALLED TO THE FIRE

# CONTENTS

## THE WHOLE MAN

Charles Johnson did not intend to be a civil rights activist. He was just being a good pastor.

He had no desire to move to Mississippi during the volatile 1960s. He did not set out to stand down the unjust systems of a segregated South, or get tangled up in a national civil rights case, or take up a mantle of activism for the African American community of Meridian. His passion flowed from a center more fiery than the furnace of racism. Charles Johnson knew that in order to be called *to* the fire one must first be called *by* the Fire.

Reverend Johnson lifted the heads of a people with little opportunity, few jobs, and no voice. The public education system failed them, the marketplace rejected them, and the justice system ignored them. While the powers-that-be worked to limit the African American vote in the public sphere, the preacher insisted each was elected to receive the love of God. They were, he assured, chosen for greatness in the kingdom of heaven and God wanted to empower their lives on earth. He worked to help *the whole man*.

Charles Johnson dignified a people by demanding justice *for* them. Charles Johnson dignified another people by demanding justice *from* them. This is the nature of prophetic speech and the effect of justice restored. Justice means to invite a healing to occur both in the life of an oppressed and an oppressor, for it is beneath the dignity of a fully whole person to treat another as a second-rate human.

Leaders like Charles Johnson are responsible for the progress our country has made toward living with respect for our neighbor. These changes did not come without sacrifice, however. The young minister soon discovered that operating out of the convictions of his heart would be costly, risky, and flat-out dangerous. Customs had to be challenged and laws had to be changed. This is now a nation of neighbors, friends, coworkers, church family, and indeed family, across lines that once divided it.

Charles has a hard time interpreting this faithful witness as heroic, however. Today, we tend to pick and choose the nature of activism for which we want to be known. For the black pastor in the South during the middle sixties, what we commonly call activism now was, then, simply survival.

*As an African American pastor in those days you were either*

*active or you just didn't care . . . weren't concerned about your peo-*
*ple. That was my philosophy about dealing with the whole man, the*
*body, soul, and spirit. If I was going to help his soul, his heart, then*
*I was going to have to work to better his whole life.*

Over fifty years later Charles Johnson is still ministering in the
same community, working for the same just outcomes and righteous rewards. He has ministered to thousands, inspired tens of
thousands, and worked to change the lives of millions. The results
of his obedience to God will continue and multiply for generations
to come.

To know Charles's story is to know the courage that is summoned in each one of us. The One who called Charles to the fire is
calling each of us to pursue justice and righteousness and to live a
life that is whole. It is a call that summons forth courage from the
heart of the fearful, redeemed relationship for the socially broken,
and trust in the One who is always faithful.

> Charles, in the telling of his story, has elected to omit or obscure
> profanity from this book, including the spelling of one of the most
> offensive racial epithets of our time. The presence of this word is
> used to illustrate some of the attitudes and hateful speech that were
> part of the social milieu during the period of struggle for civil rights
> depicted in this book.

"God at one and the same time *upholds*
a given political or economic system,
since some such system is required to support human life;
*condemns* that system insofar
as it is destructive of fully human life;
and *presses for its transformation* into a more humane order.
Conservatives stress the first,
revolutionaries the second, reformers the third.
The Christian is expected to hold together all three."
—Walter Wink, *The Powers That Be*[1]

## CHAPTER 1

# CALLED TO TESTIFY

*... let us pray God will come, in a blotting out of sectional differences and racial animosities and suspicions, in a determination to administer absolute justice, in a willing obedience among all classes to the mandates of the law. This, coupled with our material prosperity, will bring into our beloved South a new heaven and a new earth.*

~Booker T. Washington[1]

our Honor, the prosecution calls Reverend Charles Johnson to the witness stand."

A white police officer dressed in uniform khakis stepped across the hall to retrieve a "small, wiry and dark"[2] man from a privately guarded room where he and the only other African American subpoenaed in the federal trial anxiously awaited their turns.[3] From the back of the courtroom the deputy swung open one side of a wooden set of French doors that were tall, narrow, and stained a deep, dark brown. The officer self-consciously escorted the twenty-nine-year-old pastor through the center of a crowded room. All eyes turned to watch the witness enter. The place was packed with FBI agents, US Marshals, reporters, lawyers, defendants, and their supporters. The strangely jovial atmosphere turned malicious as the minister approached the bench.

Though two leaders of the African American community in Meridian, Mississippi, had been subpoenaed to appear in court for the prosecution only the minister would take the stand during the two-week trial. The exchange during his testimony would disclose a motivation in the defense so guided by bigotry and founded on falsity that it would rattle a predisposed judge and jury from their moral slumber.

Outside the federal building a large American flag waved wildly in the October sky. Directly across the street a rival Confederate flag had been temporarily erected just for this trial in front of a popular hangout, the local barber shop. It was October 8, 1967, a little more than three years after the murders of three civil rights activists drew the attention of the nation to Mississippi's Neshoba County and its neighboring community, Meridian.

What was it like to be the only African American in a federal courtroom packed with FBI agents, reporters, police officers, jurors, audacious spectators, and a row of defendants so long it spanned the front row, turned the corner, and lined the wall adjacent to the witness stand?

What was it like to sit beside a judge with a known record for intolerance of anything civil rights? Who had been cited for calling black people "chimpanzees" in public? Who discouraged the federal trial from taking place and declared the murders of three civil rights activists a crime against Mississippi, but certainly not a crime against the nation?

What was it like to sit before an all-white jury from which the bench had allowed the defense to dismiss nineteen African American citizens from the panel?

What was it like to sit before a defense team of twelve lawyers who jointly represented a line of eighteen defendants that included the Imperial Wizard of the White Knights of the Ku Klux Klan alongside the neighboring county's sheriff and deputy sheriff; the row of accused offenders treating the trial as informally as an afternoon at the barber shop, cracking jokes and snickering from behind unlit cigars?

*It was a circus . . . just one big fiasco . . .*

Three years earlier, on a sultry Mississippi Sunday in 1964, three civil rights activists drove the forty-mile stretch from Meridian, Mississippi, to Philadelphia, Mississippi, to behold the ashen remains of the Mt. Zion Church eight miles east of town. Michael Schwerner, the leader of the trio, had devoted months trying to help the African American community get politically organized and, in particular, register to vote.

The people of Mt. Zion had suffered for their activism. On June 16, the Klan burned down their church. Five days after the burning, the three activists from Meridian drove to Mt. Zion to inspect the charred remnants and attempt to console the community. The fire had been both punishment and warning to the black men and women who worshipped there. The fire was also a ploy to lure the activists to the Philadelphia area where the Klan had a stronghold on the community and had networked itself into the local police department.

Schwerner was a twenty-four-year-old white Jewish social worker from New York. With him was James Earl Chaney, a twenty-one-year-old African American native of Meridian, and Andrew Goodman, a twenty-year-old white man, also Jewish, from New York. Goodman had just arrived in Meridian the previous day after meeting Schwerner and Chaney at a civil rights training event in Oxford, Ohio, that week. There they had reviewed and role-played the fundamental tenets of Freedom Summer: nonviolent activism.

Walking among the Mt. Zion debris, turning blackened rubble over with the toes of their shoes, the three activists were deeply disheartened. For Michael, who had convinced the members of the church to host a voter registration center, this was a major setback to the mission. James Earl, born and raised in Meridian, was not at all surprised. Young Andrew was the most taken aback. He had just arrived in Meridian the night before. A plethora of thoughts must have barraged his mind, among them: "What have I gotten myself into?" This was no training event. This was the real Mississippi.

Driving back to Meridian by Highway 16 the three were stopped for speeding, arrested by the deputy sheriff, and held in the county jail in downtown Philadelphia for approximately seven hours. After their release they resumed the trip back to Meridian, physically and emotionally drained. During this final leg of a complicated trip the three young men went missing. The Federal Bureau of Investigation would scour the county for six weeks before finding their bodies buried in an earthen dam a few miles south of Philadelphia. It appeared the Neshoba County police had conspired to deliver the three young men right into the hands of their murderers.

Though nineteen men were arrested in November, 1964, for conspiring to deny Chaney, Goodman, and Schwerner their civil rights, the trial did not make its way into the courtroom until 1967, three years later.[4]

It was in this trial that Charles Johnson would testify.

When Reverend Johnson reached the front of the courtroom he was sworn in, though the expression is used loosely. This was a man devout in faith and practice. The Good Book the court asked a witness to swear on ironically encourages a believer to avoid this sort of oath.[5] When the court appealed to the minister's veracity he chose his words carefully: "I, Charles Johnson, do solemnly *affirm* to tell the truth. . . ." The court accepted his statement and the witness took his seat alongside and beneath the judge.

John Doar was the Assistant Attorney General and Head of the Civil Rights Division in the US Justice Department. He was a serious man, always found in typical federal employee attire: a dark suit, white shirt, and thin, dark tie. Seasoned by several volatile events in the Civil Rights Movement, Doar was familiar with the terrain of Mississippi policy in the 60s. He led the prosecution with aspirations to retire when it was all over.[6] This would be either a landmark case or a disappointing closure to a hard-fought battle.

Doar led Johnson through several short questions to establish the witness's character before the jury: "What is your name? Where do you live? What do you do? Where do you serve?"[7] The preacher answered with the same pith as counsel asked: "Charles Johnson. Meridian, Mississippi. Minister. Church of the Nazarene."

Doar swiftly turned the interchange to the matter at hand. "Reverend Johnson, did you know Michael Schwerner?"

"I did."

"How long did you know him?"

"February, 1964, until his death in June."

"Did you know him well?"

"Yes."

"And where did you know him? What city?"

"Meridian."

"What was his race?"

"White."

Doar addressed the witness in a matter-of-fact tone and Johnson followed suit. Wasting no time the counsel deftly summoned the nature of Charles's and Schwerner's mutual interests. "What were the circumstances of your acquaintance with him?"

"He was interested in some of the same things I was interested in, and we worked together to try to get some of these things come to pass." The counsel for the prosecution asked the minister another question and Charles continued to describe the things he and Michael had worked on together. "Voter registration, better jobs, upgrading of employment, and better education ... also police treatment of Negroes."

Johnson told of Schwerner's leadership at the Meridian COFO (Council of Federated Organizations) office located in the African American business district downtown. He told about the community organizing that went into the various efforts to establish voter registration or to secure decent work for black citizens. He explained that these committees and organizational meetings were comprised of both black and white activists working together for a better city. And when asked what Michael looked like the preacher described a casual young man in jeans, t-shirt, and a goatee.

"What kind of a beard?" interrupted the judge, leaning down toward the witness and addressing him personally.

"Kinda' a goat beard," Charles answered looking up toward the bench. This description would be most identifiable for the members of the defense who had come to refer to Schwerner as "Whiskers," referring to the tuft of facial hair he sported on his chin. The defendants discreetly cast one another knowing glances. The judge prodded the prosecution to continue.

After establishing that Michael, or "Mickey" as he was often called, had also been working in Philadelphia and greater Neshoba County to register black voters, Mr. Doar closed his examination.

"You may cross-examine," the court said to the vast team of a dozen lawyers representing the defense.

A thirty-something-year-old attorney from Neshoba County

named Laurel Weir scooted his wooden chair noisily across the tile floor and rose slowly from the table. As serious and collected as prosecutor John Doar was, the senior counsel for the defense, Laurel Weir, was lighthearted and relaxed. Weir "had established himself as something of a homespun wit in Neshoba County courtrooms and spoke in such an exaggerated country way that it was hard to believe it wasn't cultivated," recounts Florence Mars, a Philadelphia native who attended the hearings and faithfully recorded the proceedings as a concerned citizen of Neshoba County. "He wore gray suits that matched his eyes, and his hair was slicked down like a peeled onion."[8]

*He was like a bull in a china shop,* Charles later remembered.

Laurel Weir's first question would set the tone for the cross-examination. He stood behind the table centered among the dozen seated counsel. His ego, however, seemed to fill the courtroom. He crossed his arms and addressed the witness in an embellished southern accent.

"Reverend Johnson, you are a member of the colored race yourself?" he asked with a smirk on his lips. The lawyer was poking fun at the witness. He was drawing attention to the man's race with a pejorative label and belittling him in front of the jury. A couple of the defendants snickered at this first question.

Prosecutor Doar recognized the jovial condescension immediately. He was familiar with the weaknesses inherent in the attitudes of the smug and suspected this would come back to bite the defense. He was right.

"Negro race, yes sir," Charles clarified for the defense. He was not given to the humor nor slighted by it.

From this point forward Weir systematically set out to paint an unflattering picture of Michael Schwerner through his questions for Reverend Johnson. Jumping from subject to subject, he simultaneously quizzed the witness and slandered the victim before the jury. About the controversial Vietnam War of the sixties he asked if Schwerner advocated burning draft cards, then suddenly shifted gears by asking about his religious views.

"Well, he was an atheist, wasn't he?" Weir shot at the minister.

"Was he an atheist?" Charles asked in response, surprised at the question.

"Was he an atheist," Weir seemed to say again rather than ask.

"I don't know," Charles answered.

"Well, you are a minister of the gospel, aren't you?" the defense needled the preacher.

Charles began, "I didn't talk with..." but was abruptly interrupted mid-sentence with another question: "You never did go to Cuba?" In 1967, a question about Cuba was not a geographical question but a political one. Weir was implying that Charles was a Communist, that he'd gone down to Cuba to train for a Communist takeover of the United States.

"No." Charles had never left the country. He would have to answer "No" to this same question three more times before the lawyer turned back to religion.

"Now did I understand you to say that Mr. Schwerner was like Jesus or did I misunderstand that?"

"You misunderstood that," the witness answered pointedly.

Mr. Robert Hauberg, US Attorney for Mississippi and member of the prosecution, objected loudly from the table where he and John Doar sat. Charles was glad to hear another voice. It had begun to feel like he was the defendant on trial rather than a witness for the federal justice department.

Judge Harold Cox, quiet to this point, warned the defense against badgering the witness. His protectiveness toward Charles, however, could easily have been motivated by his desire to get this trial over with. He was not known for his affability toward civil rights and he did not believe this case should be tried in the federal courtroom. In his mind this affair was a waste of his time. Weir asked the judge to indulge the defense for a while longer and after receiving a gentle verbal nudge from the bench resumed his line of questioning.

Charles affirmed that he and Schwerner had advocated boycotts together and he described for the courtroom the various organizations by which the movement was operating in Mississippi. Schwerner and Johnson worked together in COFO. This was the umbrella organization that coordinated the activities of the various civil rights activist groups. When Laurel Weir asked Charles Johnson if Michael Schwerner was a member of the NAACP, Charles said he didn't think so.

"*You* are, aren't you?" the lawyer directed at the witness.

"Sure," Reverend Johnson answered quickly.

"Big member aren't you?" Weir had done his homework. Johnson was found to be a critical voice in Meridian for this national organization that was bolstered by local leaders wielding oratory skills. Reverend Johnson could preach. He could rally the saints and his growing church was quite indicative of this. Members of his church quickly became active citizens in civil rights matters if they had not been involved already. He did not shy from announcing boycotts from the pulpit, and he had no problem rallying workers from among his followers for the freedom school and other community projects.

"You're proud of it, aren't you?" Weir nearly chewed the words on their way out of his mouth.

"Yes."

"Very proud?" Weir seemed to be luring the same smug spirit from Johnson that he had claimed for himself from the start.

"Very," Johnson maintained. The preacher was calm and collected and this seemed to irritate the lawyer.

At this point the lawyer reminded the witness of the eighteen defendants sitting across from the black man, as if he could forget. "Now, of course, you wouldn't know anything about who may or may not be guilty in this case, would you? And you wouldn't undertake to tell the Court and jury that you know if any of the people on trial were guilty of anything would you?"

"Right." The pastor was too smart for that.

For the next several minutes Charles endured a barrage of questions attacking his credibility. Weir found it hard to believe Charles's greatest offense was a parking ticket, and when he noticed a skin condition on Charles's head suggested the scars were evidence he was the type to "fracas."

Weir then aimlessly meandered back to another question about boycotts, Hauberg again objected, and the judge questioned the defense, "What is the relevancy of it?" His patience was wearing thin with the proceeding.

Weir donned his most innocent school-boy face. "Well, Your Honor please...what we are trying...what is happening, of course...we have these notes passed in and in order to represent the other attorneys fairly I ought to ask that question." From time to time throughout the examination the lawyer had sifted through some notes in front of him. Weir motioned toward a disparate set of papers that contained the thoughts of twelve lawyers representing the eighteen accused.

Slightly more firm, the judge responded, gathering speed as he spoke, "I see your reason but I don't see the relevancy of it and if you don't tell me I won't know what the relevancy is."

Weir collected his thoughts scattered across the table then resumed by asking about Schwerner again: his marital status (married), living situation (apartment), and relationships with black women (unsure). The prosecution objected to the line of questioning and for the first time the bench revealed a clear lean away from the defense's strategy. "Sustain the objection."

Weir was shaken from his humor. He blinked hard, then attempted the same line with more direct examination but was stopped short.

"Objection!" came Hauberg.

"Sustain the objection," ruled the bench.

Pause. New direction. Weir shuffled through some papers,
looked up from the table and addressed the witness, again, as if *he*
was on trial. The lawyer asked for Reverend Johnson's home state
(Florida), birthplace (Orlando), and ministerial training (West
Virginia). "And then you came to Mississippi?"

"Correct," answered the reverend. How could he forget coming
to Mississippi? The decision to come to this state was the greatest
crisis of his life.

Johnson caught a look in Weir's eyes that suggested he was zero-
ing in on a target. Eyeing the witness the counsel persisted in a
thick Miss'ippi drawl, "And while you were in Virginia did you take
*special* education or courses or training in order to further the
cause that you testified you are so very interested in?"

"Just the ministry." Johnson wasn't entirely sure what else the
attorney was alluding to.

"Well, ministry and also these things that you told the prosecutor
attorney here about this voting proposition, your training, and the
upgrading, etc. . . . Did you take *special* courses and training along
those lines?" In Weir's eyes, and in those of the entire defense,
these interests Johnson had served for improving the lives of black
people had nothing to do with pastoring a church. To them the
preacher had forgotten his place and had begun to meddle in things
he ought not to disturb.

"I trained for the ministry," Reverend Johnson replied. He had
attended the Nazarene Bible College in Institute, West Virginia, in
response to what he knew was a divine call on his life. God had so

shaped his thinking and practice at Bible College that the pastor would rely on this foundation for decades to come.

The lawyer found his swagger again. He slowed his speech and persisted a third time as if to insist there was more to the story. "Well, was that the *real* purpose that you took the training... to learn these things that you are so interested in and come to Mississippi and advocate them?" He subtly offered the courtroom the notion that all this agitation in Mississippi kept coming from outside of the state. An all-white jury might "Amen" at this point. The state had a hard time shaking negative publicity throughout the sixties and even conscientious citizens had grown tired of bad press. As Weir honed in on his subject the jury would make the connection. Schwerner and Goodman were both from New York. This black preacher, trained in West Virginia, came to stir things up, too.

Charles listened carefully. He heard the insinuations. He understood well the mindset that his people had come up against time and again like a brick wall. He thought of his flock, his parishioners' needs and all the trials and suffering they'd endured long before he ever arrived. Then he clearly and prophetically answered as slowly as he was asked:

"I took my training to help *the whole man.*"

# CHAPTER 2

## A CRY IN THE DARKNESS

*A person is infinitely more than what happens to him or her, the specific events and places of one lifetime. Men and women are also the product, or prisoner of all the things that happened and were thought generation upon generation before their births.*
~Anthony Walton[1]

O n March 5, 1938, an uncertified midwife arrived at 744 Boston Avenue in Orlando, Florida. She was there to attend Martha Johnson, who was about to give birth to her fifth child. Martha labored in a small, wood-frame, three-room house that sat a tad lower than the other homes in the neighborhood. It was a little nearer the earth, slightly more humble.

*The other houses stood up on blocks. Ours sat square on the ground. One step and you were inside. The joists sat flat on the earth with only the floorboards to separate your feet from the ground. I could peek through the gaps and see dirt if the light shone just right.*

The house had a small kitchen area for preparing meals and a bathroom had been added onto the back. Well, *bathroom* may be a stretch. It was a commode that had been placed on the back porch with walls built around it to partition the occupant from view by the neighborhood.

Not a lot is known about the father, Robert. He died before his fifth child could remember him and he wasn't much talked about in the Johnson home after his death. Martha Johnson raised her five children as a single mother. If she wasn't home she was at work, sweating out long shifts at Dr. Phillips' Processing Plant. There she sectioned fruit five days a week, cutting grapefruit and oranges into portions for a modest wage. It was 1938 and meager pay had reached a critical low. On June 25 in this year President Franklin D. Roosevelt signed the Fair Labor Standards Act requiring employers to pay laborers no less than twenty-five cents an hour, ensuring a full-time employee to earn at least $10 a week before taxes. The tired mother worked hard, but they were poor.

Martha was a private person, even known at times to be a home-body. But giving birth to her fifth child would not be a private event in the African American neighborhood situated a couple of blocks east of the Orange Blossom Trail. The dwellings sat close together lining both sides of the sandy, baked-clay road.

*When someone sneezed in one house, the neighbor wiped his nose in the next! That's how close the houses felt. Nah, they weren't really that tight, but it felt like it at times.*

It's been said that it takes a village to raise a child. In those days, and in those parts, just giving birth took a village. Four small children, three boys and one girl, fell silent and wide-eyed as the mid-wife worked with their mother in one of the two bedrooms at the back of the house. The front room doubled as a living room by day and a bedroom after dark, but this night it served as a waiting room for the children and a few caring neighbors who had come to keep the children occupied, and keep tabs on Martha, and to wait.

And so it was that on a clear, Saturday night in Central Florida a baby boy cried, piercing the darkness, announcing his arrival.

Martha cried, too, but not just because of pain, or relief, or even because of joy. She cried because she knew her baby boy was entering a world already at odds with him. She cried because, for reasons she nor he nor any single person could control, he would grow up being told he was somehow less and inferior to other little boys and girls; being told he was subordinate, incomplete; separated, but without the distinction of being set apart—as in segregated drinking fountains and schools. She cried because she had introduced a soul into a world of which she was already afraid and it was her responsibility to keep him safe and protected and fed. First, Martha cried. And, then, she named her baby boy "Charles."

CHAPTER 3

# THE NEIGHBORHOOD

*It did not take me long to figure out I was a
second-class citizen. Long before I was old enough to
understand what a word like racism meant, I ran into
the reality of it on the streets of my hometown.*
~John Perkins[1]

*W*hen Phil Phillips came to the Orlando area in 1897, he had a vision for becoming the largest citrus provider in the country. Growing his empire to cover 5,000 acres in nine counties of Central Florida, his vision eventually came to include the state's first planned community equipped with a post office, railroad depot, schools, grocer, and 5,000 residents. Today the area near Sand Lake bears the name by which he is best known: Dr. Phillips.[2]

By the 1930s, Phillips Processing Plant was one of the largest and most modern packing houses in the world. Seeking a new way to market in the citrus industry, Phillips came up with an innovative way to can juice without compromising the fruit's fresh flavor and appearance. His method was called "flash pasteurization," in which he rapidly heated squeezed juice to the temperature of 180 degrees for thirty seconds, canned the juice, then immersed the cans in cold water for another twenty minutes. This method of rapidly heating then quickly cooling the juice greatly improved the flavor of the canned drink and enabled Phillips to market his product all over the country.[3]

Phillips was known to temporarily bring laborers in from the

Bahamas to work in his citrus fields. He also employed local
African Americans and eventually demonstrated his commitment to
the black community by establishing the Dr. Phillips Hospital.
While some may argue his incentive was to hire cheap labor, the
Phillips Charity nonprofit organization touts to this day that the
company's agenda has always been to better the community. Even
now the Dr. Phillips foundation advertises its commitment to "help
others help themselves."[4]

One of Dr. Phillips' faithful employees, Martha Johnson left her
five children at home six days a week and walked the five miles
across town to work a twelve-hour shift on weekdays and half a day
on Saturdays. For much of the year Martha left before daylight and
returned after, or as Charles calls it from *can't see to can't see.* ...
Although Martha kept up this grueling schedule for twenty plus
years, the Johnson family never experienced life above poverty.
The only Christmas gifts Charles ever remembers receiving were
from the veterans of the American Legion, who collected presents
for the poorest neighborhoods of the city.

Martha's instructions for her children were few, but one was
often repeated: "Stay away from white people! They'll trick you! You
can't trust 'em!"

It's easy to imagine what experiences may have furthered this
mindset. Did her employer pay black workers an unfair wage? Were
Martha and other women subject to sexual harassment in the workplace? Was the walk to and from work perilous and threatening?
Teaching her children a healthy fear of white people was one of the

ways she showed them she loved them. Her children's lives could depend on it. For a black family in the segregated South, "Stay away from white people" was as normal a warning as "Look both ways before crossing the street."

Charles was bothered, though, by the fear that consumed his mother. He saw how it compromised her life.

*The fear had gotten inside her. Mother went to work or she was at home. She didn't do much else than that. She was always afraid of what might happen. She lived a very fearful life.*

The kids had one another, they had friends, and they had the neighborhood surrounding Boston Avenue. Their street ran about 100 yards from Carter Street on the north end to a bend on the south that turned into America Street. Boston ran parallel to the Orange Blossom Trail of Highway 441 that connected north and south just three blocks west. Southwest a couple of miles was the Holden area surrounding Holden Lake. Each morning the kids walked the three miles to Holden Street Elementary School and back in the afternoon.

*Two or three miles—that was a short walk to us, then.*

This community was positioned on the crossroads of a civil collision. During young Charles's life he witnessed a great many progresses and a great many setbacks. The city of Orlando invested in the infrastructure of the African American neighborhoods, but societal pressures continued to push back and resist progress for the black community.

Improvements were made in the community during Charles's childhood. The city paved Boston Avenue. A community center was founded on the block. A public pool was dug and opened to the neighborhood. John H. Jackson was Orlando's first Black recreational superintendent. He was given oversight of the land on Carter Street to develop a recreational center. Today, the John H. Jackson Community Center still stands as a beacon of hope for children in the neighborhood.[5] In limited but important ways, community life for the African Americans living in the Orlando area was strengthened.

On the other hand, racial tension mounted during this time, too. Down the street a white store owner was openly racist and wielded control in the African American community. Ironically, his name was Mr. Black. His was the closest store that would accept credit. The community members held him in disdain, but they were also indebted to him most of the time.

Mr. Black was an officer in the Ku Klux Klan. He operated his business in the African American community, made his profit by the people, and then terrorized them from considering themselves an equal and contributing presence in the city. Charles remembers half a dozen different times during his childhood when the Klan would march down the street in front of his house. Usually there was no specific occasion for the demonstration. No particular incident had prompted the invasive parade of men garbed in white robes and pointed hoods. The Klan march was just a reminder that African Americans could be the victims of white violence at any time. The march was a reminder that all of southern society, from custom to law, protected white southerners and left black southerners at risk.

When asked if these marches made him afraid or if the Klan made him angry, Charles replied: *Both! It made you afraid, and it made you angry.* It also, of course, furthered the divide between the white and black communities, the very thing it set out to do. The African American community had little hope for responding with anything less than racism, too.

One of the great improvements to Charles's neighborhood was the community center's new tennis courts, built when Charles was about eight years old. The courts edged up to the Johnson backyard, and when the center turned the lights on at recreation time from 7 to 9 pm each night, it would light up the entire neighborhood. While he never played tennis, a young Charles is easy to imagine, as he often did, standing at the perimeter of his own backyard with his fingers curled in the chain-link fence that lined the courts.

Athletic African American men clad in shorts and tennis shoes exhibited strength and control as they manipulated the small, yellow ball beneath the bright stadium-style lights.

*That was a great thing when they did that; when they turned the lights on.*

Watching the men play, Charles had time to think. Their speed and agility made a deep impression on his young mind. Pounding up and down the court, the athletes' muscular frames glistened under the bright lights. Perspiration dripped from each limb as a player threw himself into the game, grunting on serve or gasping in a sideline dive. When the lights came on the entire community admired the impressive display of physical aptitude. This was a game of great ability but of strategy, too. The winner not only out-played his competitor, he out-thought him.

The world in these courts stood in stark contrast to the world outside. On the tennis court, nothing stopped the black man from proving his ability. All players started on the same level with zero points or, technically, "love."[6] The best player ended with the most points and with the greatest number of matches. The rules were consistent, and if an athlete wanted to improve his game he simply worked harder. The final score would reveal his hard work.

Beyond the fence of the tennis courts was another story. The black man seemed to have started the game behind in points, and the rules would often change in the middle of the game. He worked hard, but received fewer points, if any, for each victory. The game in life was inconsistent with how a fair game should be played.

None of this was lost on young Charles. Though he never played on the tennis courts or commanded the admiration and respect of the community audience—*I never played. I was a rather small fellow*—Charles was keen to the discrepancies in life. He wanted things to be different.

Even as a boy Charles was unsettled by the nature of things. His mother's exhortation to distrust whites was unsettling, too. How does one break from the mold of racism when a mother must teach her child a healthy distrust toward another people to keep him safe? When it seems the only way her child will survive is to instill fear in him from mingling with persons of another color?

One day Charles went with his older brothers to buy some groceries at Mr. Black's store a few blocks away. It was likely a reluctant, yet necessary, trip for buying merchandise by charge account. Mr. Black's son was there. He and Charles were the same age, both about ten years old at the time. The boy watched the brothers as they came in his father's store and singled out his target. He fell in behind Charles and followed closely on his heels. At one point the owner's son purposely knocked into Charles to get a rise out of him. Charles ignored it and went on.

The brothers finished their shopping and emerged from the front door with the white young man still following. Just as the bell over the door rang its closing, he fell into Charles with an exaggerated stumble a second time. Now outside, Charles turned on the boy and the two rolled in the dust, wrestling and struggling in a fight that had been started by someone else.

Mr. Black came out of the store yelling his son's name and grabbing him up by the arm. Charles was left alone in the dirt as the proprietor sent his boy back into the store. About the time Charles expected to get a lashing, by tongue or even a leather belt, the man fell silent and went back inside. The Johnson boys, though, were terrified by his silence. They picked their little brother up, dusted him off and rushed straight home where they closed the doors, drew the drapes, and waited in fear.

*We just knew the Klan was going to come get me that night. That was what happened. You could expect it for messing with a Klan-member's family. I was supposed to be hanged, killed!*

Martha was beside herself with fear for, and anger at, her children for bringing this calamity on the family. They hid with dread and bated breath through the night, alarmed by every stray dog or cat. This only served to reinforce the message Martha preached week in and week out: "Stay away from white people—You can't trust them."

But no one ever came to the house that night, and nothing came of this fight. *God sure did look after me! I was supposed to be dead....*

# CHAPTER 4

C.R. SMITH

*I have learned that success is to be measured not so much by the position that one has reached in life as by the obstacles which he has overcome while trying to succeed.*
~Booker T. Washington[1]

*O*n a bright Florida morning, a tall, young man with a slender build bent over the trunk of his car, methodically arranging its contents with care. His baby-blue Haspel suit was freshly washed and pressed, his white leather wingtips freshly polished, laces waxed. He smiled to himself as he delicately wrapped the merchandise in dark-colored felt cloth and placed each item in a safe nest of its own.

The trunk had been packed like a lasagna dish. A layer of blankets and rugs lined the bottom, then a layer of breakables, more blankets, some decorative lamps and clocks, and blankets again. Lamp shades sat in the back seat of his 1930s Ford. In the front passenger seat sat a lunch his wife, Genevieve, had packed for him, a thermos full of ice water, and a worn King James Bible.

C.R. Smith kissed his pregnant wife good-bye then slid behind the wheel of his car and rolled down the window. First he said a prayer. "Lord, open opportunities to me, today." Then he backed out of their drive and contentedly cruised the four miles across town from his white neighborhood to the historically African American Parramore area of Orlando.

As he drove, the streets narrowed and the homes grew closer

together. The palm trees remained a fixture from neighborhood to neighborhood, but the condition of the homes seemed to deteriorate. They were humble, but not cluttered. The manicured lawns in town gave way to patchy sand lots worn from the feet of the neighborhood kids' constant activity.

Driving down Carter Street, Smith passed children enjoying their summer break. A few African American boys about twelve years of age watched him turn slowly into their neighborhood. They wore the same clothes they had worn during the school year, khaki pants faded from multiple washes, and button-down, short-sleeve shirts. The color of their shirts had dulled to an earthy tone, which made the white man's suit seem even more bright and brilliant.

C.R. waved as he passed, and then stopped about a block ahead on the bend of Boston and America Street. He parked under the shade of an old oak tree and straightened from his car, stretching as if he'd been on a long drive. He smiled and waved again to the boys, this time with a shout, "Hello, fellas!" None of the boys waved back, but he held his gaze and smile as if they did.

Circling his car the man opened his trunk and pulled merchandise out one by one, holding each up to the light of the sun. He was not so much inspecting the contents as appreciating each item again. The boys watched as he wound clocks, then put them to his ear and listened for the tick. He spread open blankets, shook and refolded them. He secured shades to porcelain lamps that were formed in the shape of a horse, then took the shades back off again. He repacked each item, carefully stealing glimpses of the boys whose curiosity lured them to the shade of a palm tree about twenty yards away.

Occasionally, C.R. would look up at the boys so as to share appreciation for this fine merchandise. "How about this one?!" he seemed to express inaudibly. He'd approvingly shake his head in admiration for each piece while the boys faked their disinterest.

The truth is they were curious—but not about the merchandise. They were curious about this man who brazenly walked their streets and knocked on their doors when he could have sold twice as much twice as fast in a white neighborhood. He seemed to have no ties to the white establishments near the neighborhood and regarded everyone he saw as a long, lost friend.

When a child came to the door, C.R. would immediately get down on one knee and look deep into the eyes of the little one, talking in a kind voice and with deep sincerity. The knees of his trousers often bore the dust of that kneel for the rest of the day, darkening with perspiration and time.

In the really hot weather he'd wipe his brow with a white handkerchief then stuff it in his back pocket. It was the same one he'd use to spread over his lap at lunchtime, sitting under a shade tree or in the park where he could enjoy the sound of children playing. After he ate, C.R. would pull out the worn Bible that he took with him everywhere he went. For a while he'd read, then lean his head back on the trunk of the tree and close his eyes.

Charles couldn't figure out this white man who had become a kind of fixture in the greater Parramore area. His car was spotted at least a couple of times a week on the corner of this and that street. No one seemed to discourage the salesman, but no one really wanted to be caught fraternizing with him either. Many whites got used to seeing him travel in and out of the black community, too, and more often regarded him as a sort of nut for spending so much time there.

In the back of his head Charles could hear the not-so-gentle reminder of his mother: "Stay away from those white people! You can't trust them. They'll trick you and fool you—just don't mess with them at all." He knew his mother would never buy anything from the salesman.

But Charles found himself wanting to follow the man and observe his activity. Other salesmen had come and gone. This man was different. He seemed to have a different motivation in life. There was a happiness that spilled over onto whomever he was with, child or adult.

*What I was hearing from Mother and what I was seeing in C.R. Smith just didn't match up. As I watched C.R. I saw that he wasn't like what I had been taught white people were like. He was breaking down the stereotype for me. My walls of fear were crumbling.*

And so Charles and his friends watched the salesman from a safe distance, but they never talked to him or got too close.

One August morning the boys were loitering near the salesman's parked Ford. Looking up, they saw C.R. walking briskly toward them. They froze. Had they been leaning on his car? Did someone scratch it? He was upon them before any of them had decided to run or even act tough. Without slowing, however, C.R. swiftly snagged a set of keys from his pocket and fumbled to unlock the trunk.

"Charles, open that back seat door," he said without looking up. He knew Charles's name? Charles had never before spoken to the man. "Grab one of those shades, will you?" C.R. lifted a red lamp from behind the giant trunk lid and walked toward Charles. "That one right there," he said, motioning toward the back seat of his car, while the boy stood with a bewildered look on his face. The friends were quiet, one still poised with a marble set on his thumb he'd forgotten to shoot. Charles reached into the car and lifted the shade slowly.

"Thank you, *son,*" C.R. said as he placed the shade atop the lamp and threaded the wing nut. Charles didn't answer.

The boys hadn't noticed the woman of the house who stood behind them. "I been wantin' one of those..." she said. Smith's face broke into a broad smile as he pointed out its features and fine craftsmanship. Charles didn't really hear the conversation between the two adults, he was still hearing the word that took him by surprise, rolling it around in his head and marveling at the soothing effect it had on him. *He called me "son"*...

Reaching down, Charles picked up the cord that had fallen to the ground during the salesman's pitch and dragged in the dust. So when C.R. handed the lamp to its new owner, Charles also handed her the end he was holding.

As the customer walked home with her new lamp, C.R. turned on the balls of his feet. "We did it!" he exclaimed to the boys who still wondered if they had been too close to his car. "Thanks for your help, Charles. You make a fine assistant." His affirmation poured over the boy's ears like honey on a warm biscuit, seeping its sweetness into the crevices of his heart and mind. The other boys, too, congratulated Charles as if his assistance was what tipped the sale.

From then on the guys began to look forward to when C.R. Smith came around. They enjoyed his winsome interaction. When he parked on a certain street, they showed up. He called them by name and expressed sincere concern for their lives.

*He took an interest in us boys. He really did care. I know he wasn't really there to sell things. His business—that was just a means to an end. His primary purpose was to invest in the lives of the African American children in our community.*

Charles wrestled with what he'd been taught all his life about white people.

*It just didn't make sense in my mind. Who C.R. Smith was and who I knew white people to be just didn't align. Something had to give.*

Charles found he not only enjoyed being around this kind man, he also trusted him. As he grew older he began to work with C.R. managing his accounts and sales while he was away then settling with him when he returned. Smith's confidence in Charles boosted the boy's self-worth.

While Smith had used his business as a means of entering the black neighborhood, he then saturated the community with evangelistic fervor. He'd testify to the love of God to Charles and the other boys who hung around and then he'd live out that love in surprising ways.

It wasn't always safe for Smith. Charles witnessed the flip side of racism wielded against his white friend in the African American community. He learned of God's love by watching C.R.'s perseverance and undying love for others. Cursed and threatened by black residents, C.R. refused to desert the urban poor. As their relationship grew, Charles would be ready to brawl on C.R.'s behalf. "Now, Charles, you can't let it get to you," C.R. would say to his young friend.

*I trusted C.R. Smith. It just became very clear he loved us. I knew he loved me.*

Charles was right about the white salesman. Smith would somehow make a lifetime career of investing in the African American community of Central Florida. Mark Schlueb, staff writer for the *Orlando Sentinel,* called C.R. "the Mother Teresa of Orlando for the help he gave tens of thousands of inner-city children."[2] He proved himself time and again to the city of Orlando as being a genuine agent for positive change.

C.R. eventually moved his sales business to a warehouse, then later converted that building into a community center called Frontline Outreach. To draw kids to the center he attached a speaker to the roof of his car and blasted Christian music over it as he drove slowly through the neighborhoods. Then he'd feed kids tuna fish sandwiches and Kool-Aid. Smith did whatever he had to do to show urban youth they were loved and valued.

During the sixties, Smith started an outreach program called the Tom Skinner Club. Tom Skinner was a militant, black gang member in Harlem whose life was transformed by Christ. Smith partnered with Skinner to create a strategic ministry to black youth who were more acquainted with street life than church. Over time Smith earned the trust of hardened gang members and mediated peace on streets that formerly raged with territorial conflict. The city of Orlando recognized Smith's contributions by naming the street on which Frontline Ministries operated as "C.R. Smith Street." The mayor also declared January 31—the day C.R. was awarded for Outstanding Community Service and Better Race Relations in 1981—as C.R. Smith Day in Orlando.

Young Charles didn't know it, but Smith, who had grown up in a hardscrabble sharecropping family in rural Georgia, had a keen appreciation of the economic oppression that affected the lives of both black southerners and poor white southerners. He was a devout Christian, and, as a young man, C.R. felt a deep yearning to minister to children caught in the cycle of urban poverty. He wanted to make a difference in the lives of poor Orlando youth.

It was C.R. Smith who called the Nazarene Headquarters in Kansas City and appealed to the general church to send a black evangelist to Orlando for a revival. Smith planned to hold it in the auditorium at the Holden School where Charles attended as a younger boy. Charles was seventeen years old by now. He had known and even worked for C.R. for several years.

The black minister who came to Orlando for the crusade was a young elder named Warren Rogers. He came for one week to preach the gospel and a white couple named Tripp served as the musicians for the services. The revival was well attended by a diverse crowd in the African American neighborhood, about fifty black and one hundred white members who came over from the white Nazarene church. The integrated worship was shocking to Charles. It was the first time he had ever seen all different colors worshipping together.

It was not only the mixed-race congregation that got Charles's attention. He heard, as if for the first time, a gospel that found its completion in a life of holiness: "You can be forgiven of your sins, and you can live free from the power of sin." Charles wanted the power of the Holy Spirit to consume his being. He responded when the invitation was given and said "Yes" to the work of Christ in his life.

Charles was not the only convert won that week in June of 1955. Seventeen souls were saved in the crusade. Out of this revival began a new church called Praise Temple. A reverend named Archie Williams was sent to be the pastor and they moved into a storefront building to hold weekly services. Charles was firmly fixed in this new congregation and he soaked up the teachings of Christ in the small Nazarene church

Smith's love for Charles would become a mainstay in the young man's life, and Charles in turn held a deep kinship for his mentor. Even into adulthood Charles returned to visit C.R. at every possible opportunity and, when separated by miles, corresponded by mail, careful to close his letter to the white salesman with the affectionate farewell:

Your Son,

Charles

## CHAPTER 5

# I AM SENDING YOU

*For surely I know the plans I have for you, says the L*ORD*, plans for your welfare and not for harm, to give you a future with hope.*
~Jeremiah 29:11

harles came to Christ at about the same time he fell in love with a woman. He met and married his wife, Carrie, at the age of seventeen. They were firmly fixed in Praise Temple, and they learned to walk together as a married couple during the same years they were learning how to love and praise God.

A couple of years into their marriage Charles began to feel a nudge. He had been heavily influenced by C.R. Smith's great passion and zeal for Christ. C.R.'s spiritual fervor was contagious. Charles wanted more. He wanted obedience. He wanted to trust God and walk with God. He wanted to follow his Lord.

After thinking about it for a time, Charles decided to talk to C.R. about what he thought might be a genuine calling from the Lord.

"I think I'd like to attend the Nazarene Bible College there in West Virginia," said Charles to his spiritual mentor.

"You know you've got a wife, now…" responded C.R., suggesting the gravity of such a decision.

"I know," answered Charles. "I feel like God is calling me to do this. But I don't know if I can afford it."

"You really want to go?" asked C.R.

"I really do," responded the earnest young man.

"Well, if you can work your way through Bible school," started the businessman, "I'll get you there."

C.R. assumed the few debts the young couple had and paid for them to travel to West Virginia to start in Nazarene Bible College. There was never any question which Bible college Charles would attend. He wanted to serve in the denomination in which he'd found life in Christ, and the other Nazarene school in the South, Trevecca Nazarene College in Nashville, Tennessee, did not welcome black students at that time.

Life at Nazarene Bible College in Institute, West Virginia, was hard but gratifying. Charles threw himself into his studies while also seeing to the needs of his marriage. Working through the night as an orderly at St. Joseph Hospital in Charleston, Charles would take a bus back to Institute in time to catch class in the morning. He'd sleep when he could, sometimes between class or in the afternoon before heading to work. Sometimes he'd catch a few winks in a vacant wheelchair when things were slow at the hospital, or on the thirty-minute bus ride between work and school. When Charles could stay awake for them, the evening meals were the young couple's opportunity to connect each day.

They lived on campus with the other twenty full-time students with families and six faculty. It was a tight-knit community at the Bible College. JoeAnn Ballard, a compassionate ministry founder and director in Memphis, Tennessee, who also attended Nazarene Bible College, reflected on her experience there: "You really came to depend on your teachers. They became your parents and your family. There was a lot of trust."

In school, Charles studied church history, theology, and Bible. He also learned that the Nazarene tradition names a distinction between social holiness and personal holiness, but sees the two as inextricably linked. John Wesley, upon whose theology the Church of the Nazarene bases its holiness doctrine, was known to say, "There is no holiness but social holiness," meaning that a person's moral character means nothing if it has not been extended to the pursuit of just and righteous relationships. Or, in the words of Mississippi civil rights activist Fannie Lou Hamer, "Ain't no such thing as I can hate anybody and hope to see God's face."[1] The holiness doctrine communicated there harmonized biblical teaching with both a personal and communal responsibility to grace.[2] Holiness was expressed as whole-ness. A person surrendered to God's will is a whole person as body, soul, and spirit. The good news is that all the world can become whole, can become complete in Christ.

Charles was at the top of his class. He demonstrated an academic and spiritual fortitude to the faculty and administrators during his time in Nazarene Bible College. This was a most gratifying time in his life, a learning experience that seamlessly combined education with practice. The community of faculty and students all living together on the campus in Institute was deeply rewarding.

Upon completion of his education at the Nazarene Bible College, Charles was ready to serve a church. Near the end of his last semester of classes, he would meet with Warren Rogers, now the district superintendent of the Nazarene Church's Gulf Central District—an

ecclesial district that spanned sixteen states, encompassing all of the
African American Nazarene churches located there. The superintendent was responsible for matching ministers to the churches in
his charge, so when Charles met with D.S. Rogers he would learn
which church he would be serving in his first pastorate.

When Rogers arrived, Charles was ready. He had done his
research on the churches in need of a pastor. At the top of his
personal list was a racially diverse church in progressive San
Diego, California. The description of the assignment pinned to
the bulletin board in the college commons area captured
Charles's attention:

> Strong, mid-size church with a diverse membership and long his-
> tory. Financially self-sustaining, the San Diego church offers a reg-
> ular weekly salary and a parsonage.

Attached to the post was a small photo of an impressive church
building and another one of the parsonage. The house was a spa-
cious ranch-style home with a two-car garage attached at one end.
Charles's imagination came alive. He saw himself ministering to a
godly folk in a paradise of white sand and blue skies.

Not only did Charles know where he wanted to go he knew
where he did not want to go. There was another church open for
appointment. It was in Meridian, Mississippi. To the degree San
Diego sounded desirable Meridian sounded undesirable. It was a
small church struggling to survive on district mission money
located in the heart of the Deep South. Next to the description of

the church was a photo of the small, square building and the little block parsonage at the rear corner of the sanctuary. It looked dismal. Charles pitied the poor fellow to end up going there.

*And so me and the Lord had already talked. I told the Lord and three more folks, "I'll go anywhere but Mississippi!" That was my prayer. Because I had seen some terrible things happening there* —he shakes his head as if to shutter the national reputation of Mississippi free from his mind—*I really didn't want to be a part of it. I was afraid of it.*

The San Diego church stood on the precipice of an unending horizon while the Meridian church teetered on the edge of despair. There seemed to be only one reasonable option for where to send a capable Bible College graduate.

Over the next few days, before his official meeting with Rogers, Charles found ways to run into the district superintendent and hint about his desire to serve in California. *I dropped so many hints he had to stumble over them.*

*It came time for me to meet with the district superintendent, and I went in and I was really confident because of the fact that he knew me and we knew each other and these D.S.'s, you know, when we like each other... let's just say I knew I had right coming.*

When Charles was summoned from the other students he entered a room where the district superintendent and a couple of faculty members in dark suits sat together on the opposite side of a long table. Charles took his seat before his teachers and mentors, anxiously awaiting word of his ministry assignment.

In a deep, baritone voice the district superintendent started carefully and methodically into Charles's case: "Brother Johnson, you have done well, here, at the Bible College. You have worked hard and proven yourself in several areas."

Charles had been right about his superior's view of him. This was going to be alright. As the D.S. slowly chose his words, Charles imagined the glorious future before him.

"Brother Johnson, I am sending you..."

*Between "I am sending you" to the next statement I could envision the sea gulls flying over the ocean... I could see the white sand on the beach of San Diego and I could see all of the beautiful blue waters! And I could see myself—sometimes, when I get a break—running through the sand! I was, oh, so confident this was going to be the end of the story. I sat there waiting on the next part because I had already envisioned where I was going.*

"...I am sending you to a Utopia..." continued the seasoned superintendent.

*Hmmmm.... There wasn't but one Utopia that I knew of and that was in San Diego. I could see that picture of the two-car garage in my mind. Didn't even have a car but I wanted that garage! I could see that big, beautiful church.*

"I have a Utopia for you..."

*I could hear the drums rolling in my ear.* Charles knew the next words would be "San Diego."

Again, D.S. Rogers started over, "I am sending you..."

*By that time I felt like a peacock, my feathers—telling the* story Charles fans out his hands before him as if to display a spray of colorful feathers—*my feathers making a beautiful sight as I strutted across the chicken yard! I was happy.*

"I am sending you . . . ," said the district superintendent finally, "to Mississippi."

## CHAPTER 6

## FIRE IN MY BONES

*Let the prophet who has a dream tell the
dream, but let the one who has my word speak my
word faithfully.*
~Jeremiah 23:28

*ord, I'll go anywhere but Mississippi!* Charles lamented before God. *Father, have Thy way... but don't have it in Mississippi!*

The Bible College was in revival with a Reverend Lawler holding services in the school chapel and open to the public. At the close of one of the services Charles responded to the invitation and laid himself over the altar often known as, and certainly this time, the "mourner's bench." He wrestled over this new appointment. He simply could not come to peace with what he was being asked to do. With its intense racism, Mississippi was a place black men and women wanted to leave, not go to. Charles wept and prayed. Elders gathered around him shouting the glory down for a troubled soul. Rising from the altar, Charles knew he had more to say to God, and surely God had more to say to him. He left the chapel, went upstairs, and searched in desperation for an available classroom to pray in private. Every door was locked. The only vacant room on the second floor was the men's restroom. Charles rushed through the door without slowing to flip on the light switch. It became his closet of prayer. In desperation he prayed and wept in the darkness before the God who seemed to be calling him to do the unthinkable: to move with his young bride to the most hostile, racially segregated state in the South.

After some time of praying in this "upper room"—*It could have been five minutes, it could have been twenty*—there was a sudden spiritual collision.

Through tears of desperation, anger, and even hurt Charles poured out his feelings to God. He felt betrayed by his own brothers, sold into the hands of Egypt. How could God send him straight into the lions' den? Why would God deliver him to a fiery furnace? As he languished with the thought of marching into the fires of Mississippi, he found that his laments perfectly mirrored so many characters of Scripture. The one constant was the faithfulness of God. Every biblical story Charles knew to compare with his situation was one that ended with God keeping his servant. Joseph, Daniel, Shadrach, Meshach, Abednego... betrayal, slavery, danger, fire... God protected his people. And for each of these the confession was the same: "Our God will keep us. And even if He chooses not to we will not, we cannot, deny that our God is the Lord to Whom be praise."

The words "I am sending you" continued to reverberate in Charles's head. He could not deny the will of the Lord. This was no longer an appointment by the superintendent, it had become a commission from Christ. In the darkness, clenched fists battering the wall, he resigned his will to the will of God. "Okay!" he audibly expressed through tears dripping from his nose and chin. "I'll go... I'll go to Mississippi if that's what you want me to do!"

What happened next was a defining moment in the life of Charles Johnson. *God sanctified me in that room that day.* Charles's countenance changed from pain to praise, from anguish to joy at the nearness of the holy. In that moment God's Spirit filled the place. The room lit up with a brightness that he could not have turned on with a switch. He experienced the presence of God all around.

*It was a white light so bright!*

Charles felt the brightness permeate his soul. Suddenly, he felt a new clarity about what service to Christ might require of him, and he surrendered his heart to the call of the Lord. The desire to proclaim the gospel of Jesus Christ in Mississippi became a burning in the depths of Johnson's soul.

*It was like **FIRE**...shut up in my bones!*

A person has only to hear the voice of this veteran preacher confess such a burden to feel it deeply himself. Charles quotes another servant of the Lord to express the raw and emotional passion by which he'd been captured. The prophet, Jeremiah, struggled with his call.

"Ah, Lord GOD! Truly I do not know how to speak, for I am only a boy."

God reprimands Jeremiah.

"Do not say 'I am only a boy';

for you shall go to all to whom I send you....

Do not be afraid of them,

for I am with you to deliver you,

says the LORD."

And, later, God warns, *"Do not break down before them, or I will break you before them"* (Jeremiah 1:6-8, 17, emphasis added).

Jeremiah did as God commanded him. He proclaimed the Word of the Lord, as difficult a thing as it was for him to do. He interpreted God's intentions for God's people and spoke bravely:

"Return, O faithless children,

I will heal your faithlessness" (3:22).

"Amend your ways and your doings, and let me dwell with you in this place" (7:3).

By God's initiative Jeremiah took on the religious and social establishment of his day. He not only was unpopular among the general masses, but also among the authorities. Eventually a priest named Pashhur, who just happened to be the son of the chief officer in the house of the temple, had heard enough of Jeremiah's radical message. Feeling this jargon would upset the balance of things, and perhaps prompted by other powers that be, Pashhur arrested the prophet and had him bound in a stockade (20:1-2).

There in the stocks Jeremiah wrestled with his call, lamenting before the Lord over the difficulty and danger to which he had been summoned to serve as God's mouthpiece.

"O LORD, you have enticed me,

and I was enticed;

you have overpowered me,

and you have prevailed.

I have become a laughingstock all day long;

everyone mocks me" (20:7).

Yet, in his quandary, Jeremiah couldn't deny the fury and passion incited within his being:

"If I say,'I will not mention [the LORD],

or speak any more in his name'

then within me **there is something like a burning fire**

**shut up in my bones;**

I am weary with holding it in,

and I cannot" (20:9, emphasis added).

Charles Johnson was experiencing something of the burning passion to which Jeremiah testified. He cried and moaned and hollered a little, too. The commotion of the young man wrestling with God in the upstairs men's room reached the first floor of the Bible College building. Charles's laments had been changed to praise and he worshipped the God who answered him in his most desperate moment of submission.

Downstairs in the chapel the president of the college, Dr. Cunningham, heard the commotion of the praying student and suggested to some other colleagues, "Sounds like he's dying up there!"

*I did die that day!* Charles remembers. *That's when ol' Johnson died.*

# CHAPTER 7

## WELCOME TO MISSISSIPPI

*Too often we excuse those who are willing to build their own lives on the shattered dreams of others.*
~Robert Kennedy[1]

*T*he summer of 1961 proved to be a season of momentous journeys. Charles, a young Bible school graduate, would begin his journey to Mississippi about the same time many student activists also made significant trips into the Deep South.

The Congress of Racial Equality (commonly referred to as CORE), headquartered in Washington, DC, had strategically planned to saturate southern states with protesters. Black and white men and women defied the Jim Crow laws of the segregated south by sitting together on buses and comingling in waiting rooms clearly labeled "Whites Only." Leaving from the nation's capital they arrived at bus stations in the South where large mobs often waited for them. These activists were known as the "Freedom Riders."

Though the Freedom Riders had been trained extensively for nonviolent resistance, tensions grew as each bus moved further into the heart of Dixie. One rider remembers the trip as a public flirtation with violence. They hoped nothing bad would happen and yet they knew full well that it could further their cause if something did.

Many within the Civil Rights Movement considered the Freedom Rides too confrontational. When the first bus arrived in Atlanta on

May 13, 1961, a reception of civil rights activists awaited the Riders. Martin Luther King, Jr. was among those to greet the bus with a warning. He was concerned about the trip into Alabama. The Klan had already begun making arrangements. It was more than disheartening for the Riders to hear King admit, "I'm not getting on the buses with you, and I wouldn't go into Alabama if I were you." They continued on their journey without one of the greatest moral voices of the movement.

The very Riders who shook hands with King would be attacked by an angry mob at a bus station outside Anniston, Alabama. The bus was shaken, windows were broken, and a homemade fire bomb thrown inside. Riders were smoked out of the vehicle then brutally beaten as they gasped for air outside the bus. Eventually the police, who had been standing by the entire time, intervened.

In Mississippi, white defenders of segregation practiced a different sort of tactic for welcoming the Freedom Riders. Ross Barnett, the governor of Mississippi, saw himself as a sort of protector of Old South tradition. Anticipating the arrival of the buses, he ordered all whites to stay at home.

On May 24, 1961, the first Freedom Ride would arrive in Jackson, the capital of Mississippi. Escorted by National Guard and highway patrol the rest of the way through Alabama, a Rider remembers what he saw as they approached the state line of Mississippi. A large billboard bore the image of the state flower along with these words: "Welcome to Mississippi, the Magnolia State." The very next sign on that road read: "Prepare to meet thy God."

As the Riders entered the white waiting room the police captain was posted at the entry encouraging the blacks to "Move on. Move on. Move on." When the Riders mingled in the white section he put them all under arrest for disobeying his order. They were sent, blacks and whites together, to Parchman, the state penitentiary and most dreaded prison in the South (William Faulkner once described Parchman as "destination doom").

Rather than discourage the Freedom Riders, punishment only cemented the movement's resolve to enter Mississippi in droves. Wave after wave of public buses came to Jackson, and wave after wave of civil disobeyers were sent to Parchman. Four hundred thirty Freedom Riders would make the trek into the South, and three hundred of them would land themselves in Mississippi's dreaded penitentiary. It became a kind of gathering place for the cause; an actual teaching center for the Civil Rights Movement.[2]

On September 21, after much encouragement from the Kennedy administration toward both the activists (to back off a bit) and the state officials (to get with it), the segregationist signs were removed from the bus station waiting rooms.[3] Though the signs were gone the sentiments remained.

Such was the climate of Charles's memorable journey into Mississippi. First, though, he'd take a bus north to Mitchell, South Dakota, where he would pick up a car. Reverend Claude Dykus, a white minister, had called the young preacher in West Virginia:

"If you can come out here, I have a car for you to use in your ministry in Mississippi."

*God makes a way,* thought Charles. Leaving Institute, West Virginia, alone he traveled in the rear section of a Greyhound and then a Jack Rabbit bus to South Dakota to pick up his 1954 Chevrolet. He would drive it back to Institute to pick up his wife, pack up their belongings, drive south to Orlando for a visit to his hometown, then make his way into Mississippi.

As the miles mounted so did Charles's thoughts. *Me and the Lord had a talk all the way all those miles. "Lord, I have seen those dogs eatin' those people up ... I have seen them lock the doors, Lord ..." You've got to understand, in those days I was a scared critter!*

The week before Charles arrived in Mississippi he saw a news report of some black youth turned away from attending the State Fair in Jackson. The image of the police dogs was seared into his memory. Charles felt he didn't stand a chance. This was his destination of doom. He knew Mississippi's reputation. He had heard the stories. He'd read newspaper articles and pored over editorials in *Jet* and *Ebony*. What the news didn't report in the papers and the evening broadcasts, his imagination more than made up for.

*When I got there I looked for black people to be hangin' from street lamps!*

Charles expected to find lynching as common an occurrence as the Roman crucifixions that lined public roads in ancient days.

As the couple neared Mississippi, Charles grew more nervous. At Montgomery they took US Highway 80 toward Selma, crossing the Alabama River by way of the Edmund Pettus Bridge. From Selma and on through Uniontown the highway was flanked by occasional cotton fields, the hardened bolls just beginning to open with fibrous white pulp. It would be picking season soon.

At the state line a huge sign loomed on the side of the road with an overblown white magnolia leaf next to the words: "Welcome to Mississippi."

*Ohhhhh, my God!* Charles breathed in resignation. *I'm here.*

# CHAPTER 8

## I AM WITH YOU

*I was prepared for almost anything that could occur. I had come to feel at that time that in this struggle God was with me and through a deep religious experience I was able to endure and face anything that came my way. I think that still stands with me after a long process of giving my life to a religious way and to the will of God. I came to feel that as we struggle together we have cosmic companionship.*
~Martin Luther King, Jr.

harles held Carrie's young, tender hand as they entered the Meridian city limits on old Highway 80. Each felt the hesitation in the other but neither dared name it out loud. Entering downtown from south of town they crossed the railroad tracks that had helped to establish this as a major southern city; the Queen City it was called. Tall, stately buildings and broad streets suggested a progressive economy. Charles drove slowly through an active business district and the two were relieved to find a thriving Negro section of stores and commerce. There were no public borders, yet the newcomers could easily discern where the black business sector began and where it ended. The identifiers were subtle but certain. The white area faithfully posted segregation signs: "Whites Only" here and "Colored Only" there. A person knew he was in the black community when he no longer saw the signs.

The couple drove through the city heavy with apprehension. Black pedestrians moved about freely with apparent unconcern and this put the frightened young couple at ease. While the homes were not impressive in the black community, the mere presence of African Americans was reassuring.

After a brief survey of the town Charles counted the numbered streets higher as he traveled west and north to the address of his new church, Fitkin's Memorial Church of the Nazarene. The corner of 16th Street and 30th Avenue was a mere ten blocks from downtown. The layout of the city was easy to navigate, and the community communicated a homey, southern appeal to most outsiders.

Charles drove up to a small cement block building with a belfry. "This must be it," he said and pulled off the road onto the grassy lot. Carrie stayed in the car as the young reverend straightened from the drive and took in the sight of his new parish. A smaller square structure also made of cinder block sat adjacent to the rear corner of the church. This is where they would live. It was an unimpressive lot and Charles was mindful of the moment his feet first touched Mississippi soil. He had officially broken his promise to himself, but kept the one he made to God. Despite all his reservations he was in the Magnolia State.

Charles stood on the western corner of the grassy lot and gazed wonderingly at the bare bones structure void of life and energy.

*Standing there I just felt alone, like God had sent me and then abandoned me.*

But in the stillness of that moment, standing alone on the front lawn of his new residence and gazing toward the humble house of worship, Charles heard an audible assurance:

*I heard the words as clear as I am speaking to you: "I am with you," I heard, and as I peered up toward the sky the clouds parted, the sun shone through, and the blue sky emerged. And that was it. From that point forward I knew God was with me.*

Soon after arriving in town Charles wanted to get to the post office before it closed. District Superintendent Warren Rogers had told Charles to be sure and get a letter in the mail to him the day he arrived in Meridian. He liked to know his preachers had arrived safely so he would be free to focus on other matters of his wide-spread district. So Charles penned a quick letter once they got inside the parsonage and addressed an envelope to his superintend-ent. He couldn't miss the giant post office earlier that day as they made their way through downtown. Charles slid behind the wheel of the 1954 Chevrolet he had obtained from Reverend Dykus in South Dakota and made his way toward downtown.

The preacher crept east on 9th Street toward the federal building that housed both the US Postal Service and Federal Courthouse. Traffic seemed heavy in the late afternoon rush. As he caught sight of the monstrous concrete building, Charles eyed the steady stream of cars lining both sides of the road. The roadside parking was angled for easier entry. Heading east a driver could slide into a parking spot to the right without any problem and simply cross the street by foot to the post office. Heading west a driver could do the same and be delivered to the front steps.

Charles scanned the road for an open parking place but couldn't find a vacant space to his right. Just as he approached it, and with a clearing in the oncoming traffic, Charles made a quick U-turn left to catch an open parking spot on the north side of the street. The space was angled for westbound traffic but his sharp turn had delivered him to the space with no problem. He retrieved his letter to D.S. Rogers and started toward the broad porch of the majestic building, happy to have navigated a strange town so well. He had not made it to the second set of steps when he heard a voice holler loudly from the street.

Charles turned to see a large, white man dressed in a police uniform marching heavily toward him. He was a barrel-chested man, his red face contorted with anger. The officer seemed to cross the road in two strides to confront the black driver and unleash a torrent of curses in his face.

*He called me everything **but** a child of God...*

The Meridian City policeman had been keeping an eye on the road from across the street in Bill Gordon's Barber Shop. He was a regular in the shop even when he had no intention of getting a cut, as were others who had been passing the time there that afternoon. It was a place to read the paper and hear the news, drink coffee, smoke cigars, and tell off-color jokes. Smack in the middle of town, the place had become a kind of hub for learning the latest news and happenings. Unbeknownst to Charles, the FBI would eventually come to identify this business as a regular hangout for several members of the Ku Klux Klan. On the large picture window the words adjacent to the red-and-white-striped barber pole suggest the easy worldview adopted there: "Keep America Beautiful...Get a Haircut."

When the officer tore out after Charles, the others in the barber shop came out to the sidewalk yelling, cursing, and encouraging the policeman to "teach that ni—er a lesson!"

Towering over the preacher on the front porch of the federal building, the large policeman clenched his jaw in anger. He had seen the out-of-state tag on the black man's car.

"I don't know who you think you are! You may do that where you come from but you don't act like that around here! I'll blow your brains out, you g—d— ni—er!"

About four or so white men hollered their approval to the officer from across the street. "Kill that ni—er! Kill 'em!"

Charles's arms fell limp to his sides, his mouth agape. *Can this be happening?* He leaned back on his heels, nearly knocked over by the intensity of the moment. *Lord Jesus, help me!*

"I ought to blow your brains out!" snarled the angry officer, his hand resting on the handle of a municipal-issued revolver.

Charles's eyes grew larger as they darted from the officer to the men across the street to any passersby who might be witnessing this surreal moment, the sounds of the angry encouragers filling his head and quickening his heart.

The angry man's shoulders had hunched up and forward around his neck causing him to appear like a raging bull. After the last threat he slowly lifted his gun from the holster of his right hip.

*There we were right in front of the United States Post Office. I'm standing right beneath the American flag and this police officer is fixing to kill me on my first day in town! I could see the police report already: "Negro Killed by Officer in Self-Defense... resisted arrest... had a switch-blade." No one would question a thing!*

The angry officer stared down at the small, dark man, swearing vehemently and lifting his revolver when he suddenly stopped and fell quiet. Charles had not uttered a word. Everything had happened too fast. The officer's eyes narrowed mysteriously as if he'd seen something that caught his attention. He paused, blinked, then slowly slid his gun back down into the holster again. His livid countenance gave way to a blank stare. Without another word the officer turned and walked away.

Left gazing into a vacant skyline, Charles looked left and right then hurried into the post office to mail his letter. His tremble increased from the inside out as he processed the severity of his first encounter with the law in Mississippi. After emerging from the post office he meekly reentered his car and drove safely but quickly home.

When he came through the door, Carrie immediately knew her husband had run into trouble. Charles told his wife what had happened, his shaky hands gesturing as the angry, pointing, white men, and then the police officer pulling his gun. Carrie grabbed her husband's arms and wept at the thought of losing him. He wept, too, at the prospect that this was their new home and a new way of life for them.

From that day forward the couple coped differently with the challenges of life in Mississippi. For Charles the confrontation served as a defining moment of resolve to minister in the face of adversity. He had experienced a terrifying run-in with the area's hostility toward African Americans. Yet the conflict also affirmed the watchful eye of his Lord for him. God protected him that day, he was sure of it. Somewhere deep within he knew he had stared into the eyes of darkness and found God to be faithfully by his side. It fostered in him a supernatural, spiritual confidence.

*But God!* Charles affirms to this day. *But God! That policeman saw something, I know that. God was with me that day. "For no weapon that is formed against thee shall prosper!"*[1]

Carrie, however, absorbed every ounce of the conflict. She was devastated by this run-in with the law and wondered how they would endure living in constant fear and threat of violence. Her response to the episode was the opposite of Charles's. While he was somehow emboldened she was immobilized. Gripped by fear she refused to leave the house. From as early as her first day in Mississippi, Carrie spent her much of her day double-checking the door locks and peeking through drawn drapes.

Although Carrie was afraid, Charles became even bolder. It was as though she carried all the fear so that he could carry the courage. About six months after their first encounter Charles crossed paths with the policeman again. Charles had gone to the Corner Market on 8th Street to buy some produce when he came face to face with the hefty officer. The policeman recognized the black man he'd threatened the previous summer. He approached the young pastor and stood squarely before him looking into his eyes. "I'm going to kill you, ni—er," he growled with a deep but quiet voice that only Charles could hear. Around them in the market milled a mixture of black and white shoppers, not the kind that would yell racial slurs and death threats from a barber shop.

A surge of confidence shot through Charles at the officer's second threat on his life. This time he spoke back. "You may kill me but you can't eat me," he answered in defiance.

*I don't know why I said that—don't even know what it means. That's just what came to my mind so I said it. I was sick of his threats and wanted him to know I wasn't afraid of him.*

The officer again turned and walked away. The fear Charles had felt his first day in Mississippi was not a factor this time. He no longer feared what others might do to him. The God who sent him was the God who would protect him.

## CHAPTER 9

# FITKIN'S MEMORIAL CHURCH OF THE NAZARENE

*The sermon in a sanctified church was "loose
and formless and is in reality merely a framework
upon which to hang more songs. Every opportunity to
introduce a new rhythm is eagerly seized upon."*
~Zora Neale Hurston[1]

*T*he Johnsons were eagerly welcomed by the Fitkin's
Memorial Church of the Nazarene family. As well, interim
Pastor Roger Bowman was eager to hand over the keys and challenges of the small congregation. Many people believed this fledg-
ling church was ready to close its doors. Even the founding pastor,
Lula Williams, was pessimistic. With just a handful of children, fewer
adults, and even less money, the church was weak. The building was
in need of constant repair. A discouraged Williams was heard to say,
"We'll never have a church here. We might as well close this church
down." She packed her things and moved to Chicago. Reverend
Bowman would later enjoy reminding Charles that he had "held the
church together" for Charles until he could get there.

The tiny congregation welcomed the Johnsons with open arms.
Pastor and people greeted one another over white cake and red
punch. The entire church consisted of three adults and about ten
youth...when they all showed up. Perhaps this ratio of young people
to adults would come to shape Charles's philosophy of ministry—to
develop ministers from within the church in the years to come.

*We grow our pastors at Meridian...that's the only way we can
get 'em! We grow 'em.*

Charles quickly organized the small group of disciples to canvas the neighborhood in pairs. They walked from home to home, knocking on doors, introducing themselves, inviting neighbors to church. It was during a community saturation like this one that Charles met the woman who would become one of his all-time favorite members.

Macie Brown was a disabled, elderly woman who, after suffering a debilitating stroke, could get along only with the help of a sturdy cane. Unable to work and without a vehicle, most of her days were spent sitting on her front porch chewing snuff, hands propped before her on top of her shepherd's crooked cane. Rounding the sidewalk to climb Macie's front steps, a hock of freshly spat tobacco juice landed just shy of Charles's preaching shoes.

When he invited her to worship Macie answered, "I don't go to church…don't have a way to get there," as if in her day the only reason not to be at church was for lack of transportation. If you can get there, then there is no other reason not to be there.

"We'll come get you," said the earnest preacher.

"You will?!"

"Sure, we will!"

So she went. Macie would become a faithful member with a heart for missions. In time she served the church as the World Mission President. Fund-raising for international missions became her passion. She'd sell pecans, hold bake sales, and rally others to care for Christ's Great Commission to the church. She wanted to make sure the means were in place to send a witness to people who need Christ.

This same passion for mission work would open Charles's eyes to the vast needs surrounding him in Meridian. One day he approached the owner of the black funeral home in town, Mr. James Bishop, about helping the church fund missions overseas. Bishop was a distinguished-looking man, tall, white-haired, and often dressed in a white suit. He was a successful businessman, a leader of the African American community, and trusted by the local white officials to communicate the sentiments of black Meridian. Often officials from the city—the mayor, police chief, wealthy business owners—would meet with Bishop and other African American leaders covertly in Bishop's funeral home to discuss the role of the black community in the city.

Charles tried to garner the support of the community leader. "Mr. Bishop, could you contribute to the church and help us meet our mission budget?" the young preacher started. "Our church supports missionaries and evangelistic work in the needy nations of Africa…"

The funeral home director eyed the young preacher, "Africa?! You want to see the needy? You want to see Africa? I'll show you Africa!"

The older gentleman led the minister outside the front door of the funeral home and across the street. The two walked through a parking lot, then rounded the back of a store where a field of overgrown grass opened up, vacant but with a lone shack sitting off in a clearing. Trudging through the tall weeds Charles heard Bishop's words again as they approached the humble dwelling.

"I'll show you Africa," the older man repeated.

*The small, two-room house sat flat on the ground. It reminded me of the place where I grew up ... but worse.*

The windows were broken, doors stood wide open, and flies swirled aimlessly in the heat. Before the two men reached the front door Charles spotted several little dark-skinned bodies scurrying about the dirt yard, half a dozen children under the age of eight, running naked around the house.

*They were living in complete squalor. It was like something you'd see in a Third World country.*

The mother and father sat inside on the floor—the house was completely empty of furniture. A pile of tattered clothes was heaped in a corner, blankets for beds lined the walls and were soiled black as soot.

Charles discerned the couple hadn't a lick of education, the mother struggling to carry on a coherent conversation. The father worked a job (as a fetcher in a furniture store!), but was strung up in a cultish kind of religious group that confiscated its members' paychecks then distributed food and clothes equally among the church. Seeing the children run naked, boys and girls together, deeply disturbed Charles and he knew why his friend James had brought him here. He also knew how to respond.

*The ladies of our church went over there and cleaned those kids up, washed their hair, put clothes on them and shoes on their feet. We got them all cleaned up, fed them, and then we brought them to Sunday school and told them Jesus loved them.*

This scenario would repeat itself time and again. Fitkin's Church became a bustle of energy with many of the people that other churches neglected to reach. Poor children, wayward youth, handicapped elderly... such was the beginning of Charles's ministry in Meridian. When they didn't have the means to care for the needy, Charles went to dollar stores and grocers to ask for support. There was no person in Meridian beyond the reach of Fitkin's Memorial Church and Charles's fervency did not go unnoticed. Community leaders like James Bishop were moved by the young minister's tenacity and began supporting the ministry of the small church.

Having children in Meridian helped to root the young pastoral couple in Meridian their first few years in Mississippi. Carrie worked hard to make the house a home; however, the living conditions were not ideal for a family. The four exterior walls and the walls that divided the four rooms were all constructed of cinder block. Indoor climate control was impossible. The same block that protected them from the outdoor elements was the same block in which they tried to create an inviting interior. There was no insulation between the outer side of the brick and the inner. The Mississippi summers were hot but the winters were even more miserable. Spot heaters were used to warm the inside, but since there was no insulation between the exterior and interior of the house, a thick perspiration would film the inner walls. The warmer they tried to keep the home, the damper the air became, accompanied by the cold draft of a non-insulated space.

All furniture that sat near the wall became wet, with mildew souring the fabric. The mold spores growing inside the house wreaked havoc on the family's health, causing them to have continual colds and respiratory problems.

The church did not have the means to provide a nicer home for its pastoral family. Its worship facility was in just as bad shape as the home. Worshippers had to step over to the parsonage to use the pastor's private bathroom during services. The church was in major need of repair and was completely vulnerable to the elements. Charles often referred to the first church building as *"the place that rained on the inside when it sprinkled on the outside."* It had a belfry that leaked like a sieve. Every time it rained, the young pastor spent much of his weekend sweeping water from the foyer so that worshipers could enter on dry ground.

One Saturday Charles was sweeping the water out the door when he began to wrestle internally with his situation. His baby was home suffering with a bad cold. Charles was alone trying to salvage the church from more water damage. Floodwater had seeped into his shoes, soaking his feet. He had worked hard all week visiting, recruiting, and ministering, only to turn around and work even harder on the weekend. All the while he seemed to have so very little to show for his efforts.

Charles could not question that he had been appointed by God to

serve in Meridian. But he began to wonder, *How long, O Lord?*
Right about this time the mailman came by with the church mail.
He often would find Charles on the property and hand him the
letters personally.

"You've got a letter from Reverend Bowman," said the mailman.
Still standing in water that nearly covered his shoes, Charles
opened the letter from his predecessor.

The gist of the message: "Charles, the San Diego church is
open...thought you'd want to know. I think you'd do a fine job
out here."

Roger Bowman had left Mississippi to serve a church in
California. In time he had even served as interim pastor at the very
church in San Diego Charles had fantasized about as a student—
the one in paradise where God's favor shines down; the one where
the pastor received a steady salary and the parsonage could park
two cars in its garage. It was the church Charles had always
wanted. The excitement seemed to well up in his heart more
quickly than water in the belfry during a rainstorm...and then
Charles heard an audible and familiar Voice. It was the Voice he had
heard on the front lawn of this very same property a couple of
years earlier, assuring the minister of divine presence his first day
in town: "I am with you."

This time the Voice said, "Stay here."

And so he did.

CHAPTER 10

# CIVIL RIGHTS AND CIVIL WRONGS

*The events which will occur in Mississippi this summer may well determine the fate of Christian civilization for centuries to come.*

~Sam Bowers, Imperial Wizard of the White Knights of the Ku Klux Klan[1]

he zeal with which Charles immersed himself in Meridian ministry impressed and confirmed the Gulf Central district superintendent's decision to send him there. Reverend Warren Rogers had no doubt the appointment was a crisis moment in the life of the young minister, yet he had prayed about it as much as Charles. The area had been a burden to him. He envisioned the power of the gospel changing lives in the downtrodden black communities of the state.

Inspired by Charles's energy, the district superintendent began to hope that churches in other Mississippi towns could be revitalized. In Columbus, Mississippi, a small mission church started in the early 1940s by an older black gentleman was struggling to survive. Rogers took the young Johnson with him to Columbus to see about infusing the place with life and activity.

During one of these early trips to Columbus, Rogers and his Meridian preacher sat together in a diner catching up over a plate of southern cooking. Charles had been serving the Meridian congregation for two years by then. The D.S. asked about his struggles and the pastor willingly shared. They talked of the prevailing cultural attitude toward Negroes, and the fearfulness that pervaded the black community and kept its members from taking initiative.

As Johnson and Rogers worked their way through a meal of fried chicken livers and black-eyed peas, there was plenty of state news to digest. Rogers described for Charles the mood of Alabama following the bombing of the 16th Street Baptist Church in Birmingham that took the lives of four young black girls just two months earlier. Charles, in turn, told the D.S. about the happenings in Mississippi.

Ever since the Freedom Riders penetrated the southern states in 1961, a variety of reactions made waves through Mississippi. He talked about how the White Citizens' Councils—groups of respectable white businessmen who wanted to preserve segregation—kept black Mississippians under thumb by limiting opportunity in the marketplace. He talked about the day a young black man named James Meredith tried to integrate the University of Mississippi in the northern part of the state, and malevolent young whites sped through Meridian pelting random pedestrians with eggs in the black neighborhoods.

He talked about the assassination, in June 1963, of Medgar Evers, the Jackson field secretary for the NAACP. Charles had met Evers in Meridian during Evers's tour of the southern part of the state. There the NAACP field secretary impressed upon black citizens the importance of voter registration. Many African Americans were afraid to vote. It didn't seem worth the risk to them and their families. Black citizens were often turned away at the voting centers or persecuted for trying to register. When a hesitant citizen was talked into taking the voting registration test, she might fail the exam based on some minutiae of American history that a white proctor demanded she know. Constant opposition from the white establishment subjugated and disheartened the average African American resident from believing that change was possible.

Ever since his run-in with the police officer his first day in town, Charles had become fearless in his public initiative. He knew change was possible because he knew life beyond Meridian, Mississippi. He encouraged the community to register and began to hold training classes at church so that black citizens would be prepared for the registration exam. Some locals thought he was overoptimistic. The most discouraging of these were the local preachers who had adopted a mindset that seeking progress was futile.

Then Charles explained to the superintendent his own membership in the NAACP. "If I'm going to be a good pastor, I have to work to make life better for the people in my charge," Charles defended. "This is what we studied in Bible College. This is what y'all taught us in preparation for the ministry: to tend to the whole man; body, soul, and spirit."

"Be careful," the elder superintendent exhorted the earnest younger minister. But the D.S. did not try to talk Charles out of his NAACP membership.

The two chatted on about ministry strategy there in Columbus and simply enjoyed the rare opportunity to spend time together. Into their meal a special bulletin interrupted the programming on the TV that had previously blended into the background noise of the restaurant. It was Friday, November 22, 1963. A stoic anchorman soberly intoned from the black-and-white tube that President

John F. Kennedy was shot in downtown Dallas, Texas, while waving to cheering citizens who lined the route of his motorcade.

The two men sat in stunned silence. The world seemed to be teetering on the edge of chaos.

In his short time of pastoring Fitkin's Memorial Church, Charles grew in the eyes of the members around the all-black Gulf Central District. His church was bustling with evangelistic and social fervor. Three years after the pastor arrived in Meridian, the Sunday crowd could not fit in the tiny block building with the leaky belfry. With help from mission funds provided by the general church, Fitkin's Memorial Church was granted the funds to build a new building in 1964. That same year Charles was ordained with elder's credentials by the Church of the Nazarene. He was also elected the Sunday School Chairman of the Gulf Central District and would be attending the quadrennial General Assembly of the Church of the Nazarene in Portland, Oregon, as a delegate.

Charles's experiences as a pastor fluctuated between affirmation and discouragement. While he was a celebrated leader within the Gulf Central District, as an African American pastor he experienced the distrust of a predominantly white denomination. His church was growing in record numbers, yet he was directed by the general church to report more immediately to the white pastor of a smaller church than his in Meridian. Each week Charles had to deliver his offering to the home of the white pastor and, due to the "appropriateness of the arrangement," was instructed to walk around the house to knock on the back door of the parsonage. Whenever his church wanted to use the resources of the offerings they had raised, Charles had to petition the white pastor who held their account and mediated between Fitkin's Memorial Church and the bank. This practice only hardened the very racism Charles was fighting to overcome.

Charles's resolve for change became stronger by the day.

*As an African American pastor in those times you had to either be active or you just didn't care... weren't concerned about your people. That was my philosophy about dealing with the whole man; body, soul, and spirit.*

In early 1964 word started to spread of an upcoming saturation of Mississippi during the summer months. It would be called Freedom Summer. Six hundred volunteers, most of them idealistic students from state universities, would infiltrate the state from all over the country to promote voter registration and create educational opportunities for the African American community. A federation of activist groups called COFO (Council of Federated Organizations) began organizing strategic posts to influence change and progress throughout the state, meticulously staging Freedom Summer's activity through training conferences and carefully screening for the right volunteers.

Anticipation of this influx of activists seemed to be just the impetus to prompt a small-time vendor named Sam Bowers to begin assembling and organizing a movement of his own. Samuel Holloway Bowers, Jr., a thirty-something WWII vet who worked for a vending machine business called the Sambo Amusement Company, swiftly set about recruiting young men to his cause. His was an anti-movement aimed at thwarting the efforts of civil rights activists and maintaining a shared sense of perceived Christian values. He was on a crusade of sorts, armed with militant fervor, to preserve order and maintain power over entities, particularly blacks and Jews, that threatened the "American way." "In 1964, with Freedom Summer looming, Bowers launched his organization on the equivalent of a holy war."[2] His army was called the White Knights of the Ku Klux Klan and his enemy was anything that threatened southern white sovereignty.

The recruiting pamphlet Bowers distributed in Meridian communicated his religious and patriotic zeal:

"ONLY: sober, intelligent, courageous, Christian, American white men who are consciously and fully aware of the basic fact that their physical life and earthly destiny are absolutely bound up with the survival of this nation, under God."[3]

Sam Bowers believed that the Civil Rights Movement was the brainchild of a Communist and Jewish conspiracy operating out of

Washington, DC. He warned of an army of black men being trained by Communists in Cuba who would return to the US and take over the country. He preached white supremacy while quoting Scripture and urged young white southern men toward their moral duty in Christ.

"As Christians," Bowers communicated, "we are disposed to kindness, generosity, affection and humility in our dealings with others. As militants we are disposed to use physical force against our enemies....

"If it is necessary to eliminate someone, it should be done with no malice, in complete silence and in the manner of a Christian act."[4]

Early in 1964 one of Bowers's pamphlets landed in the hands of a bouncer at a Meridian nightclub. The passionate appeal immediately grabbed the attention and won the loyalty of the young brute. His name was Alton Wayne Roberts, the younger and even-less-composed brother of the police officer who threatened Charles's life his first day in town. When Alton Wayne met with local Klavern leader, Edgar Ray Killen—a thirty-seven year-old preacher in overalls who still lived at home with his parents—he was assured this was a society of action not just talk. "This is no boy scout troupe," Killen had said. This appealed to the raucous Roberts. He joined the Klan that spring.

Charles stood in front of the COFO office directly across the street from Young's Hotel in early 1964 with two leaders of the Southern Christian Leadership Conference (SCLC). Andrew Young and John Lewis talked with the minister about the potential of Freedom Summer in the city and commended the arrangement of the COFO office's location in the black business district of the city. Lewis was a leader in the Student Nonviolent Coordinating Committee (SNCC) and was coordinating an infiltration of six hundred student activists into Mississippi for Freedom Summer, 1964. The two men anticipated with Charles the positive influence this activism would have on the state and in Meridian that summer. Both of these men had been on that first bus of Freedom Riders back in 1961, the same summer Charles first crossed the Mississippi border.

Within the month a promising young activist named Michael "Mickey" Schwerner came from New York with his wife Rita to work at the community center in Meridian and establish the Freedom School. A passion of the Schwerners was to register African American voters in the area. The two arrived in a fury and were anxious to involve themselves in the betterment of black Mississippi. They hoped, also, to venture into neighboring Neshoba County to establish a voter registration center and a Freedom School there.

When they arrived in town the white Schwerners connected with local activists. While most ministers in town were afraid to associate with the outsider, Charles welcomed him. He fed the Schwerners "Beanie-Weenies" from a can the first night he met them. Fitkin's

Memorial Church would become a regular resting place for Schwerner and a location where he intersected with a young local named James Chaney.

Reverend Johnson turned twenty-six years old in March, 1964, a mere two years the senior of the idealistic activist from New York. Schwerner would find in Charles a common discontent with the status quo. The pastor had not resigned to the hopelessness that so permeated the black community of the South. Local African American James Chaney, the youngest of the three at age twenty-one, was also a rarity. He had gotten to the place where he simply did not care. Things needed to change. He was willing to take risks and so served as a key connector for Schwerner in the African American neighborhood, introducing the white activist to families and vouching for his credibility.

Spring of 1964 was a busy time for Charles. He was working hard for the movement and working hard for the church, which was by then involved in new construction. Civil activism and church life were often intertwined. Schwerner and Chaney helped dig the footings for the foundation of a new sanctuary for the growing congregation. Several activists scribed their initials in the wet concrete of the slab. There was constant activity around the church on 30th Avenue in those days, always something going on. If it were not for reminders that the movement was unwelcome in the city, the summer could have been considered fun.

Freedom Summer was an exciting strategy of the Civil Rights Movement. The hundreds of white and black activists that drenched

Mississippi made the twin causes of educating black children and registering black voters seem not just important, but urgent. In Meridian the community center located across the street from Young's Hotel was a fun place for young people to socialize, get snacks, and play Ping-Pong. That summer, the community center became a political center as well as a center of play and recreation. The upper level of the center housed an office and a 15,000-volume library containing the writings and influences of Frederick Douglass, W.E.B. Dubois, and Booker T. Washington. Freedom Schools were planned for the summer so that the children could advance in the learning curve and study crucial aspects of African American history that had been neglected by the public education system.

Schwerner brought a lot of energy to the local cause. Local and transplant activists began to meet almost nightly to strategize for just outcomes for African Americans. They began with a boycott of a small five-and-dime store around the corner from the community center that refused to hire black employees. After a victory there they moved on to the bigger establishments, like the Woolworth that was planted on the edge of the white and black business districts. When a young black man was severely beaten by the police department, activists picketed outside City Hall, which housed the police station in its lower level.

As Schwerner became more recognizable, his safety became less secure. He was easily identifiable with his black goatee, and several locals did not take kindly to his northern ideas. He was quickly deemed an outside agitator. For a time he and his wife, Rita, stayed in the homes of black residents. Eventually, they had to leave so as not to endanger the lives of their hosts. They had no white friends in Meridian. Threatening phone calls came in the night, bricks came through the window. They rented a house for a brief time, but the power structures made life difficult. The gas would be cut off one day, the power cut off the next, and the water cut off the next. Once in a while the Schwerners would stay across the street from the COFO office in Young's Hotel when there was a vacant room. When Rita returned to New York for a break from the struggle, Mickey stayed on the go in Meridian. Sometimes he kept moving all night long then parked in front of Charles's church at daybreak to catch some sleep in the big, long 1963 Ford Fairlane station wagon CORE had provided for the workers.[5]

Charles noticed the toll this was taking on young Schwerner. The kid had tenacity and the minister appreciated that. Schwerner didn't have to come to Meridian, didn't have to speak for African Americans, and didn't have to put himself at risk. He would have been much more comfortable at his own home, enjoying the benefits of being white. For some reason, though, Mickey was passionate about the plight of black citizens in Mississippi. He had won Charles's admiration for his efforts and sacrifice for the African American community.

In the middle of June, 1964 the newly ordained Reverend Charles Johnson boarded the train in Jackson for his first General Assembly of the Church of the Nazarene. It would take a few days to make the trip from Mississippi to Portland, Oregon, where the quadrennial assembly was being held. The national convention was held only every four years, and the young preacher counted it an honor to represent the Sunday School of the Gulf Central District and his beloved superintendent, Warren Rogers. Johnson would connect with Rogers as soon as he arrived. Until then Charles had plenty of time to reflect on the great journey that had brought him thus far.

Though Portland was just about as far as one could get from Orlando, Florida, Charles knew that he could never go so far from his hometown as he did that first day driving into Mississippi. His heart had sunk to the lowest depths. He had gone in obedience, and obedience alone. Three years later and the young preacher marveled at the watch and care of the God who had called him there. He had survived a threat on his life the first day in town, he had endured the discomfort of deplorable living conditions, and now his little church had outgrown their meager block building. The congregation had also been afforded the luxury of purchasing a nicer parsonage for the pastoral family on the same block as the church.

There was so very much to be done, but a spirit of optimism infused the black community of Meridian. Through the boycotts and picket lines and with the hope of prospective black voters they were finding their voice. COFO had primed the area for a new season in African American history.

The launch date for Freedom Summer was June 21, 1964. While Charles was traveling to Portland, Schwerner and Chaney were headed back to Meridian after attending a training session in Ohio sponsored by SNCC (Student Nonviolent Coordinating Committee). There they met up with other university student activists who would flood Mississippi to register black voters across the state. A young man named Andrew Goodman connected with Schwerner in Ohio and returned to Meridian with him and Chaney. The three were determined to implement the nonviolent practices of civil disobedience in Mississippi. Charles was halfway to Oregon by the time the threesome returned to Meridian late on a Saturday night, June 20.

A few days and several states later Charles arrived at the depot in Oregon. He placed his hat on his head, gathered up his travel bag, and stepped off the train beneath the giant 150-foot clock tower of Portland's historic Union Station. Immediately before him was a row of newspaper stands and as the minister stepped off the train his jaw dropped at the sight of the newspaper headlines that greeted his arrival:

THREE CIVIL RIGHTS ACTIVISTS MISSING IN MISSISSIPPI

The mug shots of three youthful faces, one black and two white, stared back from the front page of the newspaper. Each picture was tagged by a name. They were Andrew Goodman, James Earl Chaney, and Michael Henry Schwerner.

Federal Building that houses the Federal Courthouse
and Post Office in Meridian, MS, 2012. Photo by Chet Bush.

Charles age 10.
Photo by Janie Bell Campbell.

Charles age 19.
Photographer unknown.

OF THE

# Nazarene Bible Institute
*INSTITUTE, WEST VIRGINIA*

Recruiting Poster of the Nazarene Bible College,
circa 1960. Charles Johnson
is pictured second from the right.

Early Picture of Fitkin's Memorial
Church of the Nazarene Members,
1961. Photo by Charles Johnson.

The original (white) building and the sanctuary addition (added in 1964)
of Fitkin's Memorial Church of the Nazarene on the corner of 30th Ave. & 16th Street.
Photos by Chet Bush.

Two photos of E.F. Young Hotel in Meridian, MS, 2012.
Photos by Chet Bush.

First Union Baptist Church Sanctuary,
Meridian, MS, 2012. Photo by Chet Bush.

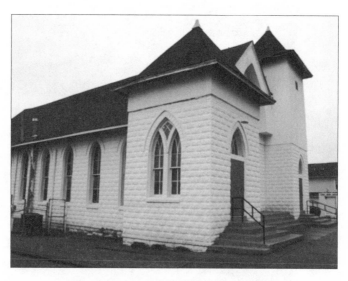

First Union Baptist Church,
Meridian, MS, 2012. Photo by Chet Bush.

Neshoba County Courthouse located in the town square
of Philadelphia, MS, 2012. Photo by Chet Bush.

Charles Johnson with Governor Cliff Finch. Photo by C.R. Darden.

March on City Hall led by Rev. Charles Johnson
on April 5, 1968. Photo by Robert Williams.

March on City Hall led by Rev. Charles Johnson
April 5, 1968. Photo by Robert Williams.

Meridian City Hall, 2012. Photo by Chet Bush.

Painting by Alton Wayne Roberts given to Rev. Charles Johnson.

Meridian Street Sign of 38th Avenue named "Dr. Charles
Johnson Ave." in August, 2011. Photo by Chet Bush.

C.R. Smith, Shirley Johnson, and Charles Johnson
at Trevecca Nazarene College (now University)
in Nashville, TN, on the occasion of Johnson's receiving
the Doctor of Divinity from the college, 1986.
Photo by Becky Combs.

# CHAPTER 11

## KING COMES TO MISSISSIPPI

*I believe that what self-centered men have torn down men other-centered can build up. I still believe that one day mankind will bow before the altars of God and be crowned triumphant over war and bloodshed, and nonviolent redemptive good will proclaim the rule of the land. "And the lion and the lamb shall lie down together and every man shall sit under his own vine and fig tree and none shall be afraid." I still believe that We Shall Overcome!*

~Martin Luther King, Jr. in his Nobel Peace Prize Acceptance Speech

*T*wo days after the three young men disappeared, the White House hosted the families of the two white activists and offered the empathy of the greater nation. Goodman's parents and Schwerner's father were with President Lyndon Johnson in the Oval Office when Johnson hung up the phone from a conversation with FBI Director, J. Edgar Hoover. "We found the car," reported the president. The blue CORE station wagon had been discovered north of Philadelphia, Mississippi. It had been set on fire then dumped in a swamp. Taking the hand of Andrew Goodman's mother, the President of the United States assured, "Ma'am, we'll do everything we can."[1] Meanwhile, James Chaney's family grieved quietly at home in Meridian.

Martin Luther King, Jr. was actively touring the South when Chaney, Goodman, and Schwerner disappeared. As time dragged on with no new information on the whereabouts of the three men, King made plans to enter Mississippi. By the time a month had passed frustrations were peaking. It seemed the inquisitive suits of the FBI and the swamp-trudging sailors of the US Navy were making a public spectacle but little progress at rescuing or recovering the bodies of the three missing men. The African

American community regarded the federal government's presence in Mississippi a debacle. They needed another voice.

It made sense for King to come first to Meridian and speak publicly before venturing into Philadelphia the next day. The African American community of Meridian was organized for progress through the leadership of clergy like Reverend Charles Johnson and Reverend R.S. Porter of the First Union Baptist Church, as well as business owners and leaders throughout the city like Connie Moore and C.R. Darden.

The "godfather" of the black community, James Bishop, owned and operated Enterprise Funeral Home where many of the major decisions of the African American community were made. Often the white city officials of Meridian would privately meet with Bishop and other African American leaders at the black funeral home to discuss matters for the welfare of Meridian. Eager to participate in the improvement of the black community, Charles attended these secret gatherings, a rising leader himself. Charles Young, the owner of Young's Hotel, would later remember how his minister friend was received by the white officials there, especially the police chief.

"Johnson may have been the only person in town who had the nerve to stand up to Chief Gunn. 'Gunn couldn't stand the sight of him,' recalled Johnson's friend Charles Young. 'When we had a meeting of some kind, Gunn would usually come. He would glare at Johnson and say, "What are you doing here?" Reverend Johnson would say, "What are you doing here?" ' "[2]

Police Chief Gunn was as cantankerous toward impropriety on the police force as he was toward civil rights. While he did not advocate black progress, he refused to allow violence in his city. In time this would come to frustrate many members of his police force.[3]

The night Martin Luther King, Jr. arrived in Meridian the city was ready. First Union Baptist Church, located eight blocks west of the southwest corner of the African American business district, hosted King's address. US marshals, FBI, and city police under federal scrutiny positioned themselves strategically around town. When Charles arrived at the church that night he looked up to find gunmen poised on the rooftops of homes across the street from First Union Baptist Church. By the time the service started, the crowd had packed the sanctuary and spilled out onto the front lawn. Speakers were wired outside to carry the message of the civil rights leader into the streets.

The traditional looking, white-brick church had begun to serve as a center for civil rights activity long before King's arrival. The Reverend R.S. Porter and Reverend Charles Johnson had convened there on several occasions to lead local activists in public demonstrations downtown. Its stately cathedral-like appearance and arched windows distinguished it within the African American community. It stood as a beacon of glory among harsh economic realities.

Inside the church oak-stained wooden pews filled the sanctuary.

Behind the wooden furniture of the platform, a vast set of brass pipes for an old pipe organ fanned the wall and created a heavy backdrop to the speaker of the service. Though windows lined the length of the auditorium on the north side of the building, the wooden furniture dampened the brightness inside. From the platform Charles surveyed the massive crowd. Shoulder to shoulder, a thousand or so people crammed into a four-hundred-seat-capacity auditorium, shoving the Mississippi July heat from their faces with funeral home fans and eyeing the visitor who sat to Charles's immediate right.

"I'm tired..." resigned the greatest moral voice of American civil rights privately to the Nazarene preacher. Charles understood Dr. King not to be talking about the demand of the day so much as the demand over the last few years that had launched him into the public arena as the voice for southern civil rights. "I'm tired... but I'm in too deep to stop now." King, also, seemed to have resigned to a greater call; the call of God, and the need of a people.

Charles answered Dr. King encouragingly, "You have an awesome responsibility which I know makes you tired. The many things that you're involved with, the many fronts you are taking care of are enough to make the strongest tired. Thank you. We appreciate that."

Seated next to the monumental activist, Charles was mindful that he had witnessed this man ten months earlier address two hundred thousand marchers in Washington, DC. Watching the event from his black-and-white Zenith television set in Meridian, Charles had heard King herald "I Have A Dream" from the steps of the Lincoln

Memorial. Charles was moved by the message but had his doubts
that this was anything he'd be seeing in Mississippi anytime soon.

*I felt it was good to hope for, but I couldn't see it happening
beyond where he was (in Washington, DC)... not in the South,
especially. My mind had been oppressed by all that was happening
in the South, and how the hostility and how the anger flowed so. I
couldn't see it, black men and white men walking and sitting
together. I couldn't see the children being counted for the content of
their character as opposed to the color of their skin. What I knew
was: Because we were black we had to stand back. I knew it was
good for him to dream but it was for us a long time coming.*

Though Martin Luther King, Jr. had advanced to the global stage
of political activism, Charles considered this event in Meridian to be
about something much more immediate than the civil rights leader.

*We all knew why we were there. This was about the three boys
that were still missing.*

While the crowd waited for the speaker, a chorus of "Ain't gonna
let nobody turn me 'roun" filled the auditorium. "I'm gonna keep on
awalkin', keep on atalkin', marchin' up to freedom land." Reverend
R.S. Porter stepped to the historic pulpit of the church he served as
pastor. He thanked the many who came out for the rally, prayed an
eloquent prayer, then introduced the special speaker of the night,
Dr. Martin Luther King, Jr.

Johnson recalls the address as not a typical King speech. The
SCLC leader did not default into one of his popular sermons by
which he is known today. He continued to press the point that these

boys needed to be found and that the events of June 21 should come to light. We can be sure he stressed the primary tenets of his activism, the impetus for going to a place where wrong had occurred, and bringing attention there: "Injustice anywhere is a threat to justice everywhere," King reminded the world.

In the middle of the fight, though, Reverend Johnson had his doubts that real change was on the way. Perhaps his friends' disappearance had dealt a critical blow to his confidence in a brighter future. Given the despair of the African American community at the time, moments like these were often perceived as less than historic.

*The importance of the whole thing was not in my mind at the time. I didn't know this was the beginning of a change for a people. At that time this was simply about the three young men missing.*

Charles also did not know then that in a mere four months King would travel to Oslo, Norway, to receive the Nobel Peace Prize where he would refer to the events of Philadelphia, Mississippi, in his acceptance speech. He eloquently described the condition of racial strife in the United States.

> I accept the Nobel Prize for Peace at a moment when 22 million Negroes of the United States are engaged in a creative battle to end the long night of racial injustice.... I am mindful that only yesterday in Philadelphia, Mississippi, young people seeking to secure the right to vote were brutalized and murdered. And only yesterday more than 40 houses of worship in the State of Mississippi alone were bombed or burned because they offered a sanctuary to those who would not accept segregation....
>
> Therefore, I must ask why this prize is awarded to a movement... which has not won the very peace and brotherhood which is the essence of the Nobel Prize.[4]

At the close of King's Meridian speech a round of applause broke out and another old spiritual swelled in the humid sanctuary before Meridian leaders stepped to the podium to encourage citizens in other local initiatives. Elections would be coming up and there was still time to prepare for the voting examination and try to get registered, one leader prodded. After a few statewide candidates were named who might benefit the African American community, Charles stepped to the pulpit to address the local economic strategy. He named the businesses that refused to hire black employees then informed the gathering that he had acquired an old cash register from a store.

*These were not normally available to us in the black community.*

Charles offered register training at Fitkin's Memorial Church for those interested in applying as a cashier at a grocery store.

After the service Charles and ten or so Meridian leaders piled into a few cars and followed behind a police escort to the Holiday Inn on Highway 80. Collaborating with King's entourage about twenty African American men dressed in dark suits gathered in the lobby of the hotel where Charles watched a line of white police officers border the entry way and windows. The armed policemen stood with their backs to the hotel entrance and kept a watchful eye toward the street, many of them Charles knew to be as racist as the day is long. This night, however, they were posted as guardians of a people they frequently threatened.

It was an odd experience and one Charles knew not to expect the day King left town. Martin Luther King, Jr. certainly had risen to an esteemed political level and his visit did garner attention for the local cause. At a time when the investigation of the events on June 21 could have drifted off the chart of public priority, King's words nudged the federal government to stay the course. Robert Kennedy, US attorney general and brother of slain US President John F. Kennedy, called Martin Luther King, Jr. while he was in Meridian to assure the community that the search for these three men would remain a priority of the US Justice Department. King reported the details of the call to the local leaders over a catered meal in a Holiday Inn conference room.

The very next morning Charles traveled with the Meridian leaders, Martin Luther King, Jr., and his entourage the short forty miles up Highway 19 to Philadelphia, Mississippi. Again, about twenty of them congregated together in the heart of town to retrace the last known steps of James Chaney, Andrew Goodman, and Michael Schwerner. Charles had no way of knowing they had already driven right past the buried bodies on the way into Neshoba County.

Congregating outside the jail on the east side of the town square, Martin and a few of his men went in to talk with local police. Charles stayed outside and talked to a few black residents who had gathered. King sized up the cells where the men had been detained and fed a Sunday supper. Chaney had been kept apart from Schwerner and Goodman, placed in a cell with another black prisoner. Segregation would be strictly adhered to even in jail. The civil servants at the prison maintained the story that the boys were released about 10:30 pm the night of June 21 and were last seen driving home toward Meridian. This continued to be a matter of contention with those most concerned about the outcome of that night since the blue station wagon the activists had been driving was found not south toward Meridian but twelve miles north of Philadelphia in the Pearl River.

Neither Charles nor Dr. King nor any of the others were comforted by this trip. More questions emerged, fewer answers were resolved. They walked around the square, which is the heart of commerce in small southern towns. Squares of the South are typically built around the central presence of the courthouse. This was true of Philadelphia, too. The county courthouse is a kind of emblem in the South, either an icon that survived the presence of Union soldiers during the Civil War, or a target of their plundering. Many courthouses were burned to the ground as Union troops advanced to their next location.

Ending their time together in front of the Neshoba County Courthouse, Charles stood among the other black leaders as King exhorted his Mississippi brethren to valiance. "Three young men came here to set you free," he told the assembled. "Things are going to get better.... Walk together, children. Don't get weary."[5]

By now the black men milling around town had elicited some attention. Random pedestrians had begun to congregate and observe as did Sheriff Lawrence Rainey and Deputy Cecil Price. Conspicuously surveying the small town, the African American leaders attracted an audience of white bystanders. Four carloads pf FBI agents watched from a distance as King spoke with his followers.

Charles knew they were acting on borrowed time, there in

Philadelphia's square, and that under other circumstances they wouldn't have gotten away with gathering together in the middle of town like they did.

*I could feel the animosity in some of the whites, and the hesitation in the black locals. I felt that if we don't ever do it again we did it this time. We came up there without fear. Before the killing of those boys we would have been thrown in jail for showing up in a group like we did. But we did it this time.*

About that time a voice hollered from the crowd: "Is this that Martin Luther Coon?" The jeer was received by a host of laughter, and the black leaders began to disseminate from the premises. It was clearly communicated that they were not welcome, even with the attention of the nation on the small town.

*We were not welcome there at all. As they started to gather around we knew it was about time to go. The federal marshals and FBI were watching us from a distance, but that's it—from a distance. The citizens that gathered around let us know they didn't like us coming in their town and bringing attention to things there.*

Two years later, on the second anniversary of June 21, Dr. King would return to Philadelphia for what he described as one of the most terrifying days of his life. An organized march was planned to end at the familiar Neshoba County Courthouse to raise awareness to the fact that still no justice had been served on behalf of the three murdered activists. Though nineteen[6] men had been arrested for conspiring to deny Chaney, Goodman, and Schwerner their civil rights, no federal judge in Mississippi had yet recognized the indictment as a legitimate federal case. The grand jury rejected the indictment three times before the trial of October, 1967, when Judge Cox received a heavy lean from President Johnson.

Assembled before the courthouse for exhortation and prayer, the three hundred or so marchers were soon surrounded by a crowd of local residents. Again, the sheriff and deputy were right there in the mix. Martin encouraged the hearers to expect justice to be carried out. Adding fuel to the hostile reception, King chided, "I believe the very murderers could be right in our midst." Without missing a beat, Deputy Cecil Price mumbled behind the speaker, "You're d— right…They're right behind you!"[7]

The surrounding crowd began to get hostile. A garden hose was turned on the marchers, bricks were thrown, and a string of firecrackers was set off. Pick-up trucks with young toughs in the back careened alongside the assembly, one jumping off a moving truck into the crowd, taking a few to the ground with him.[8]

When he left Philadelphia, Mississippi, that first trip in 1964, King told Charles and the other leaders from Meridian, "This is a terrible town. The worst I've seen. There is a complete reign of terror here."[9]

On August 4, 1964, forty-four days after the search began, J. Edgar Hoover's FBI unearthed the bodies of the three activists in an earthen dam south of Philadelphia in Neshoba County. As news spread, reporters arrived at the hospital to capture the image of Deputy Cecil Price aiding the delivery of the three body bags to the morgue. African American leader and funeral director, James Bishop, was called upon to carry the bodies back to Meridian. Only Chaney's body remained in Meridian. The bodies of Schwerner and Goodman were sent north to their families. Compelling images and video of Chaney's funeral can still be found in which his younger brother, Ben, is seen standing with his parents tearfully singing "We Shall Overcome...someday."

Charles could not attend the funeral. At the time he was out of town attending the Gulf Central District Assembly in Memphis, Tennessee. For many years to come he would speak at the annual memorial service held at Chaney's grave.

James Earl Chaney's body now rests alongside a curvy road outside Meridian on the way to the Okatibee Baptist Church. His grave sits on the edge of the cemetery and a good distance from all the others. The large tombstone has received the afflictions of both hostile emotion and careless affection. An oval indention in the headstone is now empty of the picture of the twenty-one-year-old son of Meridian. The aperture for the once "eternal flame" has been divested of its fire. A large steel frame has been erected to support the headstone that was once torn from its resting place and tossed in a nearby pond by vandals.

Occasionally fresh flowers are brought by visitors from afar who set out on pilgrimage to witness for themselves the reality of this historic nightmare. Over James's bruised bones are inscribed the words that capture the essence of lives lived in distorted pursuit and the courage of those who risk a new way of being:

THERE ARE THOSE WHO ARE ALIVE
YET WILL NEVER LIVE.
THERE ARE THOSE WHO ARE DEAD
YET WILL LIVE FOREVER.
GREAT DEEDS INSPIRE AND
ENCOURAGE THE LIVING.

## CHAPTER 12

# MERIDIAN ACTION

*The Powers are good. The Powers are fallen.*
*The Powers must be redeemed.*
~Walter Wink[1]

$\int$ ollowing Freedom Summer, and after the bodies of the three activists were found, Charles feared activism in Meridian would begin to wane. COFO did a good job of gaining the ear of the federal government, but Meridian still struggled. The movement had lost the CORE director transplanted from New York and his most loyal and brazen local. With the deaths of Schwerner and Chaney, Charles was afraid the local civil rights movement in Meridian would lose momentum.

Realizing the need for local advocacy of African Americans, Charles sensed a new conviction burning within. Several civil rights organizations had been active in Meridian—Congress of Racial Equality (CORE), National Association for the Advancement of Colored People (NAACP), Student Nonviolent Coordinating Committee (SNCC), Southern Christian Leadership Committee (SCLC). But all of those were national organizations, and Charles believed that Meridian needed a local voice that could represent the people of the city and organize them to accomplish specific gains in the black community.

So Charles Johnson started the Meridian Action Committee. This organization picked up the banner for civil rights in Meridian, continuing to call for voter registration reform, boycotting unjust businesses, and creating training programs to get workers employed in better paying jobs. The Meridian Action Committee was also an answer to the terrorist agenda of the Klan and other white supremacist groups. While many of these things had already been taking place in Meridian through COFO, the black community of Meridian found in the Meridian Action Committee (MAC) a voice and an identity unique to the concerns of their city. MAC brought greater focus to justice interests, locally persuading businesses to hire black employees and speaking out against police brutality.

One of the Meridian Action Committee's first major victories was the boycott of the Cinderella Slipper Shop. This was a shoe store that made all its business from the black community but had no black employees. One day an African American woman was shopping there when she and the white manager got into an argument over something. Their disagreement escalated until the manager assaulted the woman with a slap that sent her sprawling to the floor. The Meridian Action Committee quickly formed a boycott demanding that the manager be fired and some black employees be hired. For seven straight days men, women, and teenagers lined the sidewalk of 5th Street carrying signs that declared "THIS BUSINESS DISCRIMINATES AGAINST NEGROES." They received immediate attention. Company executives traveled to Meridian from Louisiana to meet with Charles and the boycott leaders. In response to their demands the manager was fired and a black manager and clerk were hired.

Another popular case concerned the Help-Yourself Grocery
Store. There were four such stores in town. Ninety-eight percent of
the store's clientele were African American but 100 percent of the
employees were white. Advocating for black workers, Charles personally addressed the manager one day about hiring just one black
bag boy.

"No, this is a family business," he answered Charles. He would
only hire family members and close friends. But when Charles
questioned him a little further, "What's the harm in hiring just one
black employee? Just a bag boy?" the manager became more
adamant and revealed his true colors. "I'll close down before I hire
one black worker!"

Charles and the MAC supporters showed up with their signs.

*We didn't actually call it a boycott. We used the phrase "selec-
tive buying."*

When MAC picketed one of the stores, the other three followed
suit and hired African American employees, too. Indeed, there was
a ripple effect throughout the city. Businesses began to fear boycotts greater than whatever fear kept them from hiring equally.

Charles remembers the Winn Dixie boycott as the most poten-
tially hostile. This was yet another business location that made 95
percent of its profit from the black community yet refused to invest
back in the community by offering jobs to black citizens. Charles,
again, addressed the manager first about hiring some young
women to serve as cashiers. When the supervisor rejected a
reasonable petition, MAC took action. Charles and his team of

picketers showed up with their signs beyond the edge of the parking lot near the street. They were not alone. The Klan turned out in full robe. The hooded antagonists fell in behind the picketers, bearing down on them as they tried to circle together, then hurled insults and derogatory comments at the black picketers, trying to incite them to violence.

*They were following so closely on our heels, just trying to stir something up. I had some guys who wanted to retaliate with the Klan. "That's not the way," I told my guys. We never had any violence. We kept the peace.*

Great gains were made in the workplace, but these actions did not necessarily make life easier for the black community. While MAC worked to provide more job opportunities for African Americans, many entities resisted black progress and opposed the efforts of black leaders.

To help supplement his own income, Charles found work in addition to the church that kept him in touch with the needs of the community. His first job was as an assistant instructor in Adult Basic Education, a federally funded program teaching adults how to read. The education system had failed the black population and the ratio of adult illiteracy was staggering to the Bible College graduate. The effect that poor education had on black families was troubling and he witnessed the root of poverty that plagued the Deep South. Yet, there was great resistance from the local community toward bettering the educational opportunities for black citizens.

Charles's second job in addition to pastoring was as the county project officer for the Headstart program. This was a program funded by President Lyndon Johnson's "Great Society" initiative, giving underprivileged preschool-aged children a leap on education. Charles had a difficult time finding locations to house the program. Headstart policy required a space of thirty-five square feet per child and a fenced-in yard where the children could play. The city and county schools were the best location to house the program, but both school boards refused to accommodate the program and rejected the federal funding. Hosting Headstart would have deseg-regated Meridian's public schools.

Since the school districts would not allow Headstart on their cam-pus, Charles turned to the next best place to educate underprivi-leged children, the churches. Only a few were large enough to accommodate the program. They were the First Union Baptist Church where Dr. King had come to speak, Newell Chapel (Methodist Episcopal), and Mt. Zion Missionary Baptist Church.

As the Meridian Action Committee punctured the veneer of the marketplace and federal funding bolstered educational opportuni-ties for black citizens, secret and covert attacks were systematically leveled against black leaders and their initiatives. Whereas Charles and other leaders sought to bring the issues into the public sphere, these reprisals continued to occur under the cover of darkness.

Two of the locations used for the Headstart program, Newell Chapel and Mt. Zion, were targets of the Klan. In the middle of the night a delivery man planted a box of dynamite equipped with a timer alongside an exterior supporting wall of Mt. Zion Missionary Baptist

Church. By the time it detonated the plant-man was long gone and the structure was reduced to a pile of rubble. The Newell Chapel parsonage was set aflame by a gasoline bomb, lighting up the night sky and sending a plume of black smoke to hang heavily over the city. The local Jewish community spoke out in solidarity with the African American community against the bombings of these churches, and their Temple Beth Shalom was bombed during the night.

When their facilities weren't being attacked the leaders in the African American community suffered verbal assault. Charles regularly received threatening messages and calls to his home. When he answered the telephone at three or four in the morning, concerned it could be one of his parishioners in need, he'd hear an angry voice on the other end of the line. "Ni—er!" they'd say, then hang up. This continued for years. After Martin Luther King's assassination, the threats became more specific: "Keep it up and you'll be dead like King!" Harassing phone calls came at all hours of the night, sometimes one after the other for several hours.

*I hated to do it, in case one of my people needed me, but sometimes I just had to take the phone off the hook. That was the only way we could get any rest.*

These midnight calls only furthered the extreme anxiety that had come to plague Carrie's life. When Charles was away from home she would answer the phone to hear, "If your husband keeps this up he'll wind up missing!"

*She got the calls threatening to kill us and blow us up, and she just broke.*

"I didn't marry a preacher," she reminded her husband who was torn by both the welfare of his family and obedience to the call of God.

*I had to obey God. I had to stay here.*

There was another African American minister in the Meridian phonebook with a first initial of C. and the last name of Johnson who refused to get involved in civil rights activity. He wanted no part of it and thought it would only stir up trouble. "That's none of my business," he told Charles when Charles invited the minister to participate in Meridian activism. When Reverend C. Johnson's Methodist Church was set on fire by a gasoline bomb tossed through a window in the middle of the night, the black community surmised this pastor had been confused with Charles, whose church was actively participating in the Meridian movement.

*They didn't care enough to know who they were bombing!*

Perhaps this misfire was the motivation to land a more precise attack on Charles's home. His house on the corner of 17th Street and 29th Avenue was located on the opposite corner of the same block as Fitkin's Memorial Church. The Klan pinpointed his home and planned to bomb it.

As a leader in the African American community, Charles was part of a local protection plan. Several Baptist deacons had gathered together to serve as watchmen, posting themselves in twos at the homes of leaders they knew had a target on their back. The First Union Baptist Church pastor, Reverend R.S. Porter is remembered as a tough man who "liked his rifle."[2] His deacons all carried shotguns to protect the African American leaders of Meridian around the clock. Women prepared sandwiches and sweet tea for the guards. Few protection groups of this kind operated in the South. While small, Meridian's was diligent and successful. In Louisiana there was an organized "Deacons for Defense and Justice" that operated during the 1960s. "This Meridian group was so informal it did not have a name, but its members had guns and courage."[3]

Charles was out of town the night two watchmen posted at his house spotted the white truck pulling up alongside the Johnson driveway on 17th Street. It was around one in the morning, long after delivery hours. A white man emerged from the truck carrying a shoebox-sized package and snuck up the driveway under the carport attached to the side of the house. As he crouched to place the package against the wall, his eyes met the exit end of a double-barreled shotgun. One of the deacons had rounded the corner from behind the house just as the man arrived at the carport, clicking each hammer as he lowered the gun's barrel between the bomber's eyes. So startled by the unexpected encounter during his midnight escapade, the white man began to regurgitate at the sight of the guards. He was an older man with thinning hair and a frail frame. Collecting himself, he backed away from the watchmen, making surrender motions with his hands and apologizing for being there.

"He's not staying," said the second deacon. "Let him go."

The terrified terrorist returned quickly to the van, taking his package with him.

*Those deacons saved my family's life and protected my house.*
*We had to really look out for one another in those days.*

All of the worry that Carrie internalized took a terrible toll on her health. She could not participate in activism with Charles for fear of leaving the house. It was hard for her to connect with others consumed as she was by such anxiety. A condition that she never struggled with in Florida or West Virginia completely incapacitated her in Mississippi. She became sickly and frail, and her life was cut short by the tumultuous atmosphere of the 1960s struggle. Though no one ever caused her direct physical harm, the hatred and racism, the threats of violence to her family, and despairing conditions of the African American community contributed to Carrie's physical demise. When she died a young woman during this tumultuous period, the doctors explained the cause to be congestive heart failure. Charles, however, knows that it was terror that killed his wife, and he laments her death accordingly:

*We lost her in the war.*

## CHAPTER 13

# DYNAMITE TRIAL, PART 1

*Because it is a Christian, fraternal and benevolent organization.*[1]

~Reason #1 on a leaflet detailing "Twenty Reasons WHY you should, if qualified, join, aid and support the White Knights of the KU KLUX KLAN of Mississippi" circulated by the KKK in Mississippi in 1964

hree years would elapse between Schwerner, Chaney, and Goodman's murders, and the trial of their murderers; but finally, in 1967, the trial occurred. Charles Johnson was on the stand, a witness for the Federal Justice Department.

Charles had endured the meandering harassment of the "homespun lawyer" for nearly twenty minutes on this the first day of the federal trial. He found it best to avoid the contemptuous stares of the eighteen defendants sitting opposite him along the rail and turning the corner down the wall. The belligerent counsel for the defense, Laurel Weir, however, was impossible to ignore, pelting the minister with personal attacks and innuendos that had veered far from the matter at hand.

Why, the lawyer wanted to know, had he gone to study at the Bible College in West Virginia? Hadn't all that study really been undertaken with an aim toward coming down to Mississippi and rabble-rousing? "Was that the *real* purpose that you took the training...to learn these things that you are so interested in and come to Mississippi and advocate them?"[2] the lawyer asked in an exaggerated southern accent.

"I took my training to help the *whole man*," responded the black minister in complete sincerity. What happened next in that court-room would expose the nature of injustice to its core, unveiling a sub-versive contempt that masqueraded as righteous regard for society.

Weir zeroed in on a particular matter that he had waited to intro-duce. Standing in the center of twelve lawyers sitting at the defense table, he scanned over the disparate set of papers spread across the large, oak table. With the tips of his fingers of one hand, he straightened a small page that looked to have been torn from a notepad and tapped on it twice before speaking.

"Did you ever, uh…" he corrected himself, "did Mr. Schwerner ever advocate that white women should be raped?"

There, he had said it.

Before Charles could respond, Robert Hauberg quickly inter-jected from the prosecution table, "We object to that, if the Court please." The question had taken the entire courtroom by surprise, yet it was ambiguous enough to merit some explanation, evidently. "I did not understand the question," said the judge.

"I say, you told about some of the things that Mr. Schwerner and yourself advocated…" started the lawyer, fixating on the witness. "I believe when you first talked with the prosecuting attorney and tes-tified you left off the fact that you advocated boycotting didn't you?"

It had been a long time, now, since senior prosecutor Doar had questioned Charles.

"But you told me later that you did that too. You remember that, don't you?" asked the defense lawyer accusingly.

Charles did not answer, the two of them locked in silent stare.

Weir continued, "Now, let me ask you if you and Mr. Schwerner didn't advocate and try to get young male Negroes to sign statements agreeing to rape a white woman once a week during the hot summer of 1964?"

Hauberg shot from the prosecution table again, this time louder, "We object to that, if the Court please!" No response.

*Have I heard this right?* Charles asked himself in disbelief. He grew stiller yet, the muscles throughout his body stiffening. "I believe you will have to repeat that, sir?" he stated as a question. The lawyer may have understood the rationale for such a question but to Charles it had come completely out of left field.

The reverend's heart began to quicken as the defense sought to link Charles to the fantasy that Schwerner advocated rape. Sexual impropriety toward a white woman was the fastest way to muster animosity toward a black man. Accusations of rape were typically the impetus for spontaneous lynchings. Many an African American male has been executed without trial by a Mississippi community based on such a groundless accusation.

This lawyer was not only seeking to discredit Schwerner, but to loop Charles into decades of fantasies white southerners entertained about black-on-white rape. Weir continued, exuding more confidence as he spoke, "I ask you if it is not true, and I want your answer, that you and Mr. Schwerner didn't try to get young Negro males to sign statements that they would rape one white woman a week during the hot summer of 1964 here in Mississippi?"

The question was completely ludicrous to the Nazarene minister. "No, never," he answered quickly, his face hard and unyielding.

Before the lawyer could offer a follow-up, the judge, who had presided distantly over the affair, became visibly irritated. "Counsel, you ought to have a good basis for a question like that. It would be highly improper—I hope that you know—to ask such a question without a basis for it. I'm going to look forward to seeing some basis for that question in this record," Judge Cox asserted agitatedly.

Weir raised and opened his palms as he pled with the judge, "Your Honor, please, it's a note that was passed to me by someone else."

"Well, who is the author of that question!" The judge grew angrier as the indecency of the question settled in on him.

"I don't know, sir," replied the lawyer glancing either way down the table hoping for a response.

His ignorance incited the bench. "Well, I want to find out right now who the author of that question is!" The judge's speech quickened. "Which one of you passed that question up?" Cox scanned the row of lawyers.

One of the defense team, a Mr. Alford, spoke up, admitting complicity but unwilling to bear the guilt. "It was passed to me, Your Honor, and I passed it on to him," he gestured as if passing the scratch note to Weir again.

"Who wrote that question? Whose question is it?!" fumed Judge Cox loudly.

A combination of confusion and fear issued through the defense. Each looked shamedly to his neighbor as if to respond, "Not I, Lord." Several whispers passed through the defendants to the table of counsel.

Alford spoke up again, this time offering more information, "Brother Killen wrote the question, one of the defendants." A gaunt, ashen-faced man of about forty raised his hand as his name was called. He sat among the other defendants. Ray Killen was a backwoods preacher from Neshoba County hell-bent on ridding the state of indecency. He was a stoic man in public but vociferous from the pulpit.

The judge glared at the defense. "One of the defendants wrote the question?" He shook his head in disbelief. "All right, I'm going to expect some basis for that question since Counsel has adopted one of the defendant's questions and if there's no basis for it, when we get through I'm going to say something about that.... I'm not going to allow a farce to be made of this trial and everybody might as well get that through their heads including every one of these defendants right now!"

The prosecution seemed to breathe a sigh of relief as if to say, "Finally!" Charles, though, couldn't believe his ears. The judge had indicated no sympathy toward the case of the prosecution. The trial seemed a formality, paperwork, to lay the matter to rest and let the state of Mississippi move on.

The Neshoba County lawyer was taken aback. "Your Honor, please. I will be more careful from now on about the questions I ask and I do beg the Court to understand that on this particular occasion I was trying to be diligent in obeying the Court's orders, you know."

"I don't understand such a question as that, I don't appreciate it, and I'm going to say so before I get through with the trial of this case." Judge Cox demarcated the lines of decency in the justice system. "So you can govern yourselves accordingly and you can act just as reckless as you want to in asking questions like that. Go along!" he cajoled sarcastically. The precedent had been set, though, like never before and the defense realized it had crossed a critical boundary.

All humor was lost on the defense side of the courtroom. "Your Honor, please, may I confer with associate counsel to see if there are any additional questions that they want to ask?" Weir offered, seeking a chance to regroup.

"Yes, sir," said the judge, but he continued to vent his irritation with the query. "I'm surprised at a question like that coming from a preacher, too! I'm talking about Killen, or whatever his name is..." Cox flipped his hand as he blew off the veracity of the defendant's claim.

The court went into recess and Charles was excused from the witness stand. Returning to the prosecution table, he was greeted by handshakes and assurances from John Doar and Robert Hauberg. They were not a smiling group, but they were hopeful that the precedent set in this cross-examination would color the rest of the trial. They were right. One member of the Neshoba County Board of Supervisors would later reflect on the two-week trial, "The judge got mad that first day, and stayed mad the rest of the time."[3]

# CHAPTER 14

## THE DARK NIGHT

*Whoever listens to a witness becomes a witness. In other words, you will become our witnesses.*
~Elie Wiesel[1]

harles would not take the stand again in the case of the *United States versus Cecil Price et al*—otherwise known as "The Mississippi Burning Trial"[2]—but for two days he returned to the same guarded room where he had been retained before his testimony. He was free to leave the room from time to time, use the restroom, get a drink, meander down to the post office—but he could not leave the building. The hours ticked by like years. Outside the window he could see that the Confederate flag waving large across the street at the barber shop was joined by a host of other smaller rebel flags. Drivers flew them from their car antennae and the area was flooded with Confederate supporters.

The third day into the trial, Johnson was released by the prosecution. "We won't call you to the stand again, Reverend Johnson," said the stoic Justice Department representative.

*John Doar was all business all the time.*

"Thank you for your service. You are free to go home. We'll call you if necessary."

"I think I'd like to sit in on the proceedings," said the witness.

"You can do that," responded Doar.

Slipping into the back of the courtroom, Charles nodded to a few

FBI agents eyeing his entrance and took a seat near the center aisle on the back row behind the prosecution. Several family members of the defendants began to make their way into the courtroom and quickly turned their heads when they saw the black minister seated on the spectator side of the rail. His was a very different perspective of the proceedings than the first day. It almost seemed his time on the witness stand had been a dream. He was easy to identify, again the only African American in the room, and the defense one-by-one noticed then tried to forget his presence.

Over the next several days the prosecution set out to recreate the context of Sunday, June 21, 1964. A number of witnesses were called by the federal team, among whom were several Klan informants that had been paid by the FBI to testify against the secretive sect of terrorism. The first Klan informant was Sergeant Miller of the Meridian police department.

Charles's former suspicions gave way to a disheartened countenance. His face grew heavy as one by one familiar community names and faces paraded before him as Klan members. He was not surprised, but saddened.

*I passed that man in the street just the other day. That one called me by name in public.*

As more evidence was released it seemed the truth did not become more obvious, but even more hidden. *Who else harbors malice against me and my people?* Details were unveiled, yet the sinister reality of systemic evil becomes darker and more covert the more it is known. The circle of influence widened as the story unfolded.

Sergeant Miller identified Preacher Killen, the man who passed the note that accused Reverend Johnson and Michael Schwerner of advocating the rape of white women, as the organizer of the Meridian "Klavern"—a term used to identify a local Klan assembly. While the police officer had been the first citizen of Meridian sworn into the secret society by Killen, he would be followed within a few weeks by a new group of inductees, among whom was the young tough, Alton Wayne Roberts.

Alton Wayne was a prime candidate for the Ku Klux Klan. Raised in the home of a poor Meridian sanitation worker, he caused trouble everywhere he went. At 6'2" 250 pounds he was usually found on the delivery side of a bloody fight. In high school he stood out on the football team as a furious tackler, but was let go from the team by the coach as a liability due to his temper and unchecked rage. After high school Alton Wayne was dishonorably discharged from the United States Marine Corps for drunkenness, fighting, and taking leave without permission. He returned to Meridian, got married, and had three children. Family life also failed to settle the troublemaker.

Alton Wayne had two brothers. There was Raymond who during the trial busied himself with the waving of a large Confederate flag outside Gordon's Barber Shop across the street from the courthouse. And there was Lee who served on the Meridian police force and was known to cuss out and threaten the lives of African Americans while he was on duty. Lee Roberts was the cop Charles had encountered his first day in Mississippi on the very federal property on which this trial was taking place—the cop who had called Charles *everything **but** a child of God* and threatened to kill him.

A high school teacher remembers the one act of grace expressed by Alton Wayne in his life. During class a young girl fell to the floor in a sudden diabetic seizure. The teacher was beside herself and, at a moment when no one quite knew how to respond, Roberts swept the girl up in his strong arms and ran to the principal's office where the school nurse could tend to her. Though he was proud of this act of kindness, it proved to be the one exception. It seemed the young man had no idea how to channel his energy. Some people are said not to know their own strength. Alton Wayne Roberts seemed to know his; he just didn't know what to do with it. As an unwieldy southern white man aimlessly struggling for an outlet in the volatile 1960s, Roberts and the Klan combined to create a perfect storm.[3]

From the rear of the courtroom Charles could see the backside of Alton Wayne's head among the other seventeen defendants. The story to be told those next few days connecting the horrid events with the very characters sitting before him would startle and repulse the young pastor. Each day he heard more than he wanted yet returned the next with an insatiable appetite for the truth. This is what Charles heard as the prosecution revealed the events of that dark night of June 21, 1964:

June 21 was a Sunday, Father's Day actually. Mickey Schwerner, James Chaney, and Andrew Goodman traveled the forty miles north of Meridian to inspect the charred remains of the Mt. Zion Church outside of Philadelphia. More than twenty African American churches would be fire-bombed in Mississippi that summer. Mt. Zion was the first. After visiting the property where the blackened tin roof lay crumpled from the heat on the brick foundation, the three stopped by a few African American homes in Independence Quarters, hoping to bring a victim of the church beatings back to Meridian to file a signed affidavit of the attack. They were unsuccessful in luring any church members back with them, some still in very bad shape from the battery they'd received five days earlier.

By 3 pm the civil rights workers were mindful they needed to get on the road. They had established 4 pm as the time by which they would check back in at the COFO office. If they didn't return by then, activists at the Meridian office and supervisors in Jackson would know they had run into trouble. The three piled into the 1963 blue Ford station wagon provided by CORE and took Highway 16 that traveled into Philadelphia. This would deliver them to Highway 19 where they could then turn south toward Meridian.

Cruising over the brown, baked highway on a hot, midsummer day in Mississippi, Chaney drove, the one African American in an integrated automobile, a southern no-no. Riding listlessly with the windows rolled down Schwerner and Goodman ducked when they passed a police car. A police report documented Deputy Cecil Price as recognizing the CORE station wagon and radioing excitedly, "I've got a good one!"

Just inside the Philadelphia city limits Price, who had narrowed the lead of the blue wagon to a few feet and was tailing Chaney closely, propped a spinning red light on his dash and honked repeatedly. If Chaney considered making a run for it an ironic turn of events thwarted the thought. One of the brand new, oversized Firestone tires CORE installed on the Ford specifically for navigating rural Mississippi roads went flat. Chaney pulled off at a wide spot in the road.

If he hadn't seen the white passengers before, the deputy recognized the lead civil rights "agitator" immediately. Michael Schwerner was easily identifiable with his dark goatee and round, boyish face. Price radioed for backup, then watched as the three replaced the flat tire with a spare. While they worked under the blazing afternoon sun in 100-plus degree temperature, the deputy informed the trio that Chaney was being arrested for failing to slow to thirty-five-miles-an-hour inside the city limits, and the other two were being held as suspects in the burning of the Mt. Zion Church.

Two highway patrolmen arrived to assist the local officer. Price had one drive the CORE station wagon with Chaney as his passenger, and the other drove the patrol car with Schwerner and Goodman in the back. The officer who drove Schwerner and Goodman later testified that he often took off his gun belt in hot weather and kept it in the back seat of his patrol car. When he realized he wasn't wearing it and had two prisoners in custody he turned around to retrieve it. "Schwerner either had to sit on that .357 Magnum . . . or pick it up. He had picked it up and was handing it to me, just to do me a favor. I guess that's the first time a prisoner ever handed me my own gun," the officer reflected.[4]

Price led the procession to the jail in Philadelphia. There all three were booked as "Negroes,"[5] and led to their cells. Chaney was separated from the other two and placed in a cell with another black prisoner by the first name of Cotton. Schwerner and Goodman were locked up together partitioned from the Negro cell by a thick wall. No phone call was ever made to alert Schwerner's wife, Rita, or the other CORE officers of their whereabouts. The young men grew anxious as they realized their colleagues had no idea where they were.

As the hours ticked by the arrest seemed to buy time as opposed to settle an investigation. Considering the two white men had been arrested on the grounds of suspicion in the church burning, it was odd that no interrogation ever took place. Just as odd, given the intense training these activists had come through for enduring police brutality in small southern jails—they had been told that "in Mississippi, jail and beatings were inseparable"[6]—not a hand was laid on the three.

Meanwhile, back in Meridian word spread quickly through a certain group of men assembled by Preacher Ray Killen that three civil rights workers were in the Philadelphia jail, one of them "Whiskers"—the nickname the Klan used to refer to Michael Schwerner. After gassing up two cars and purchasing some gloves from a grocery store, eight men belonging to the Meridian Klavern traveled into neighboring Neshoba County. Alton Wayne Roberts rode in the car with Preacher Killen. Afraid he might be too highly suspected, Killen had the men drop him off at a Philadelphia funeral home and the men received further directions once they met up with fellow Klansmen from Neshoba County at the courthouse downtown.

After the three men had spent more than six hours in the jail, Deputy Price decided Chaney could pay his speeding fine and the men could make their way back to Meridian. Unbeknownst to the three prisoners the phone rang at the jail while they were still locked up. It was answered by an attendant who assured the CORE director from Jackson on the other end of the line that no one had seen hide nor hair of any "Civil Rightsers." Chaney borrowed $20 from Schwerner to pay his ticket and the three piled into the Ford Fairlane station wagon to head home. It was about 10:30 pm when they left the jail.

"See how quick y'all can get out of Neshoba County," said the deputy. They thanked him and left. Deputy Price and another officer followed them closely out of town.

When the assembly of eager men milling around a gas station on the outskirts of town saw Price's car pass by on Highway 19, they quit arguing over who would pull a trigger and tore out after the patrol car. Price had already turned on his red, spinning dashboard light and was closing in on the bumper of the blue Fairlane again. For ten miles the driver led a fast-paced chase then finally pulled over, probably at the behest of the more seasoned and rational COFO leader, Michael Schwerner.

A mob of men with guns quickly surrounded the car. They forced the three to get into the back of the deputy's cruiser then drove north back toward Philadelphia before turning onto a rural, clay road south of the city limits. One of the men followed behind in the CORE station wagon. By the time the caravan of cars stopped on Rock Cut Road all restraint had been exhausted. The lynch mob was eager to inflict damage.

Alton Wayne Roberts was the first to run up to the police car. He opened the back door of the cruiser, pulled Schwerner from the car and spun him around. With his left hand grasping Schwerner's shoulder and a pistol pointed at his chest, the husky Roberts confronted the activitist, "Are you that ni—er lover?"

Schwerner, always given to reason, started to respond in his typical empathetic demeanor, "Sir, I know just how you feel." Roberts shot him through the heart. He then returned to the car, dragged out a stunned Goodman and shot him through the chest. This was Andrew Goodman's first full day in Mississippi. He fell into the ditch on the side of the road next to his friend.

Just after the shots a trailer salesman named James Jordan ran up to the scene, begging, "Save one for me!" Chaney was pulled from the police car. He immediately began to back up, pleading for his life. Jordan shot Chaney in the stomach, lamenting to the others, "You didn't leave me nothing but a ni—er...at least I killed me a ni—er." Roberts followed Jordan's shot with a few more, firing into Chaney's back and head as he lay on the dirt road.

Grasping each by the ankles and wrists, the men then shoved their victims into the back of the Ford Fairlane in the order they were killed, their bodies piled on top of the jack and flat tire they had changed just earlier that afternoon. A Philadelphia mechanic named Billy Wayne Posey got behind the wheel of the blue station wagon and told the others to follow him, "I know where we're going." They took several back roads to the Old Jolly Farm where an earthen dam was under construction. Dumping the bodies in a hole scooped out by a bulldozer, they were buried under several layers of red clay fifteen feet deep.

As they watched the bulldozer push the Mississippi soil over the three bodies, diesel fumes filling the humid sky, the men swore one another to secrecy, one vehemently exclaiming, "I'll kill anyone who talks, even if it was my own brother!" The plan to burn the station wagon was communicated and by the time the gang of men left the dam site it was nearly one thirty in the morning.

The next day each man returned to his normal routine as if nothing unusual had happened. They were husbands, fathers, and military veterans. They lived in everyday homes and went to work at everyday jobs. Among them were a mechanic, a salesman, a policeman, and a preacher.

## CHAPTER 15

## DYNAMITE TRIAL, PART 2

*I must commend the Federal Bureau of Investigation for the work they have done in uncovering the perpetrators of this dastardly act. It renews my faith in democracy.*
~Martin Luther King, Jr.

*T*hroughout the trial the Justice Department representative who led the prosecution, John Doar, treated each witness, whether for the prosecution or for the defense, with the utmost care and patience. He was a model of respect when handling a cross-examination, careful not to condescend to any person before the jury of Mississippians.

Laurel Weir, on the other hand, seemed not to have learned his lesson on the first day. He continued to exude open biases and to badger witnesses for the prosecution. One such FBI informant, a handsome, young Methodist preacher, who had joined the Klan but became disillusioned by their constant swearing, surprised everyone in the courtroom. None of the defense suspected the neat, blond, twenty-seven-year-old to be an informer of Klan activity. During a cross-examination Weir questioned the minister's character for having been paid by the FBI for the information. In typical derisive fashion he asked, "But you were paid for the information.... And instead of 30 pieces of silver you got $15,000?"

The courtroom burst into laughter but the judge did not. "Counsel, if we have any more quips like that I'm going to let you sit down," he warned.

Each time the judge reprimanded the defense for its misbehavior in the courtroom, Charles became more confident this judge wanted to do what was right. Through the course of this trial he had watched the judge's demeanor toward civil rights change dramatically.

*I went to court feeling like the judge was against civil rights matters because of what he'd said about African Americans before and his opinion toward the Federal Justice Department. But by the end of the trial I felt that Judge Cox wanted to do right. He truly wanted to uphold justice. I knew he wasn't just putting on a show for anyone, because there weren't any other blacks there to show off for, just me.*

Doar exposed the Klan's plot to murder civil rights activist Michael Schwerner with the aid of several more witnesses, not least of which was the confession of the second shooter himself, James Jordan. Schwerner's "elimination" had been authorized by Imperial Wizard Sam Bowers and widely discussed in several gatherings. The plan was put into motion the night members of the Klan traveled to Mt. Zion and posted themselves at the exits of the church. Alton Wayne Roberts was one of those who beat church members on their way out of the building. When the church was empty Roberts was reported to have raised his bloody knuckles in triumph. Testimony confirmed that the subsequent burning of the church that night was a ploy to lure Schwerner and other civil rights activists back into Neshoba County.

Florence Mars, a Philadelphia citizen who carefully documented the trial, noted that Doar was especially masterful in his closing remarks. He spoke to the jury "in a relaxed and intimate way, as if there were no one in the entire courtroom but himself and the jury." He explained why the federal government had assumed the role of prosecution in this case and encouraged them not to understand this occupation as an invasion of Philadelphia or Neshoba County. "It means only that these defendants are tried for a crime under federal law in a Mississippi city, before a Mississippi federal judge, in a Mississippi courtroom, assisted by Mississippi courtroom officials, before twelve men and women from the state of Mississippi. The sole responsibility of the determination of guilt or innocence of these men remain[s] in the hands where it should remain, the hands of the twelve citizens from the State of Mississippi."[1]

Charles had been very impressed with John Doar from the beginning of this investigation until the moment of these closing arguments. Charles thought back to their initial meetings three years earlier when the Federal Justice Department representative first approached him. They had met in the COFO office southwest of downtown in the black business quarters. Doar treated Reverend Johnson with the utmost respect and courtesy, a white man showing such due regard for a black man. Charles was not used to this.

*This was a white man communicating the message in Mississippi that a black man is worth something. He represented my government. That made me feel proud of my government. I don't know if I was proud of Mississippi, yet, but I was proud of my government. I was proud to be an American.*

As the Justice Department director reiterated the plot to eliminate Schwerner in his closing remarks, Doar identified the role of
each defendant in the evil scheme: "There are the master planners,"
he pointed, "there are the organizers, there are the look-out men,
there are the killers, there are the clean-up and disposal people, and
there are the protectors. Each of these defendants played one or
more parts in this conspiracy." Typically quiet, Doar raised his
voice when pointing out Deputy Cecil Price, triggerman Alton
Wayne Roberts, and Imperial Wizard Sam Bowers.

"If you find that these men are not guilty of this conspiracy it
would be as true to say that there was no night time release from
jail by Cecil Price, there were no White Knights, there are no young
men dead, there was no murder. If you find that these men are not
guilty you will declare the law of Neshoba County to be the law of
the State of Mississippi." The jury, representing twelve diverse communities across the state, listened intently.

Each of the twelve lawyers for the defense closed with a statement. The first was Mike Watkins, a Lauderdale County lawyer. He
offered that the deaths of these three could very well still be a publicity stunt hatched by an authority far away from Mississippi. Then
he appealed to the jury's state pride. "Mississippians rightfully
resent some hairy beatniks from another state visiting our state
with hate and defying our people. It is my opinion that the so-called
workers are not workers at all, but low class riff-raff, that are misfits
in our own land. If the people of Mississippi need help in solving
our problems we'll call upon those who are capable of helping. We'll

not send for a bum to help manage our finances or Communist to save our government."[2]

Florence Mars documented the final remarks of each of the defense with whom she shared a home community, and some of them a bloodline. "When Lawyer Weir slowly walked to face the jury he stood proud and transfixed, as if he had just come down to the front of a church to confess that he had been saved from eternal sin. With a look of transcendence on his face, and in his slow, deliberate country drawl, Weir began: 'A great burden has been lifted from my heart after hearing that the government didn't have any more evidence in this great talked about thing and that the tarnish has finally been removed and has been cast out that had been cast on Neshoba County, Mississippi. It has finally and at last been removed. Ladies and Gentlemen, I thank you from the deep of my heart for sitting here and hearing this evidence in this case, and I think the United States of America owes the people in Neshoba County an apology after they have publicized our county, and then come up here with no proof whatsoever, other than what they hire somebody to say.'"[3]

The burden of proof, Weir insisted, was on the federal government and it had failed the system. "The government must prove that these three people who are said to have been killed, I say they ain't even proved who's been killed beyond a reasonable doubt, but if they are they must prove that they are citizens of the United States of America before you could return a verdict of guilty and I haven't heard of a single witness to get up on the stand and say that

Schwerner, Goodman or Chaney were citizens of the United States of America, and if there is any reasonable doubt in your minds as to that effect, you should find them not guilty."[4]

One by one the defense paraded a line of tangents and distractions before the jury, each as sincere and heart-stricken as the next, treating the twelve Mississippi representatives in a deeply spiritual Sunday-go-to-meetin' sort of way.

Following the lengthy procession Judge Cox exhorted the jury to carefully discern a verdict in the case. He stated the definition for conspiracy and reviewed the terms in which a person participates in that conspiracy. Dismissing the jury on a Wednesday afternoon, the twelve deliberated together into the night, resumed the next morning and continued into the afternoon.

When Charles left the courthouse Wednesday afternoon, he knew how to rally his parishioners for their weekly Wednesday prayer meeting. They would be praying, among other things, for justice, for truth to come to light, and for the evildoers to face judgment. While the preacher was plenty confident in the Lord, his confidence in the jury was waning. He did not expect a guilty verdict.

During the deliberation of the jury the defendants cut up with the same jovial condescension with which they had treated the entire affair, cracking jokes and being raucous in the halls of the federal building. A picture was posted in the *New York Times* of Edgar Ray Killen and Cecil Price proudly hailing the front page of a newspaper with the bold headline: VERDICT BY JURY AWAITED. Killen grins boyishly while Price hooks a giant stogie with his forefinger beneath a wide-rimmed cowboy hat. The eighteen defendants seemed to travel the extra mile to communicate an air of conceit.

*I really expected nothing. The way the defendants were laughing and carrying on during the trial, winking at members of the jury, tipping their heads like they knew one another. The judge didn't see that part because he was looking at the lawyers doing the talking. But I was watching them. I was looking. And even though I knew the case had been presented properly—and you couldn't miss it, the truth—the Klan was a powerful thing in this area then and I didn't know how many of those jurors were sympathizers. I expected nothing to be done.*

More than twenty-four hours after they had been released from the courtroom, the jury returned on Thursday afternoon to report they were unable to reach a verdict.[5] Charles was not surprised. But, rather than declare a mistrial, Judge Cox sent the jury back into deliberation, an act commonly referred to in law as the "Dynamite Charge." Judges gave a Dynamite Charge when they wanted to stress the importance of a decisive verdict. Judge Cox told the jury that the deaths of Schwerner, Chaney, and Goodman were too important, too hot, to remain unresolved. "It is your duty as jurors to consult with one another and to deliberate with a view to reaching an agreement..." he pressured.

Outside the courtroom the defendants continued their hurrah in the federal halls. "Judge Cox just gave the Dynamite Charge.... We've got some dynamite for him ourselves, haven't we?!" Wayne Roberts joked to Cecil Price.

Charles was not present the next morning, Friday, October 20, when the jury returned to announce their verdict. The minister hadn't expected the jury to return so soon this time around, so he took his time making his way to the courtroom that morning. By the time he arrived at the federal building on 9th Street, reporters with cameras around their necks and notepads in their hands were scurrying down the broad steps of the portico. "Guilty!" he heard among the hustle of the press.

Of the eighteen defendants, seven—including Deputy Sheriff Cecil Price; Imperial Wizard of the White Knights of the Ku Klux Klan Sam Bowers; and the hotheaded bully, Alton Wayne Roberts—were convicted of conspiracy to murder. Eight of the eighteen were acquitted, among them Neshoba County Sheriff Lawrence Rainey. Three, including the backwater, segregationist preacher Edgar Ray Killen, drew mistrials.[6]

Charles entered the lobby of the federal building outside the post office where he encountered John Doar and his staff. The two men gripped hands and affirmed the word to one another again: "Guilty?" "Guilty!" Exiting the tall front doors of the federal building Charles stood aside while reporters aimed short, staccato questions at the federal agent.

Doar answered, "These men were found guilty by fellow

Mississippians. This speaks volumes against the Klan's activity in this area."

*I was so excited. I was excited that our government cared. We were a cared-for black people. You just don't know. That our government would send its best lawyers down here with the backing of the US government and say, "You commit the crime, you'll do the time," and not stop short because it was black people. Some people said none of that would have happened if two white boys didn't get killed, but I didn't have that attitude. I was excited. John Doar impressed me a lot.*

Above the minister waved a large American flag whipping wildly in the October sky.

The case was a turning point for Mississippi. "This was the first time a jury in the state had returned a guilty verdict in a major civil rights case...and the convictions marked the end of the long chain of widely publicized and unpunished racial killings that began after the Supreme Court decision of 1954."[7]

Charles joined the prosecution team of seven or so as they strolled through downtown toward the black business district and landed at a favored restaurant of the out-of-towners, Albert Jones's Steakhouse. Several of the press corps had congregated here by now, too, and Charles marveled at the lighthearted atmosphere.

*I remember sitting there around that table with the men and women, all of them smiling and talking. There were other people already there and the atmosphere of our table just spread through the restaurant. The word "Guilty" was carried out into the streets. A big group congregated there at Albert's, almost like a church meeting. Fifth Street just lit up when they heard the news.*

CHAPTER 16

## A VERY DISMAL DAY

*We can move in that direction as a country, in
greater polarization; black people amongst black,
white people amongst white, filled with hatred toward
one another. Or we can make an effort, as Martin
Luther King did, to understand and to comprehend,
and to replace that violence, that stain of bloodshed
that has spread across our land, with an effort to
understand compassion and love.*

~Robert Kennedy in an Indianapolis campaign speech the night of Martin Luther King's
assassination[1]

*O*f course, the murders of civil rights activists did not end with the Mississippi Burning case.

On a stormy Wednesday night in April 1968, a tired Martin Luther King, Jr. stepped to a podium to exhort a gathering of Memphis sanitation workers who were on strike for improved benefits as employees in a black-dominated service. He arrived late and was feeling under the weather. Toward the end of his speech he slid into a familiar, melodic sermon encouraging his followers to seek American freedoms with or without him:

> ...I don't know what will happen, now. But it really doesn't matter with me, now. *Because I've been* to the mountaintop. Like anybody I would like to live a long life, longevity has its place. But I'm not concerned about that now. I just want to do God's will. He's allowed me to go up the mountain. I've looked over and *I've seen* the Promised Land. I may not get there with you but I want you to know tonight that we as a people *will get* to the Promised Land. So I'm *happy* tonight, I'm *not worried* about *anything,* I'm *not fearing* of *any man. Mine eyes* have seen the glory of the coming of the Lord!

At the close of his sermon King was received into the arms of his brethren who toured the nation in pursuit of just outcomes.

That same day escaped-convict James Earl Ray scoped King's motel door from the window of his own Memphis hotel room, and waited for the African American leader to emerge. The next evening at approximately 6 p.m. Ray dropped King with a single sniper bullet through the neck. He wrapped the murder weapon in a blanket, stowed it in a random doorway of a back alley, and fled Memphis.

The American voice of nonviolence had been silenced.

There are days we do not forget in history. Charles remembers the feeling he had when he heard Dr. King had been assassinated.

*It felt like the bottom fell out of the world.*

The killing of King was an act against more than one man. It was an attempt to silence a people; to silence a message. Among the plethora of activism, Dr. King's message was the one most threatening. He led a movement, not militant but resilient. He expressed a message, not violent but persistent. He called for peace, brotherhood, and relationship. This is dangerous. This threatens the balance of power that is based on superiority and control. The man was quieted, but the message was not.

Charles quickly assembled the Meridian Action Committee. He knew the wisdom of the African American leadership would determine the nature of the communal response. *Your leadership will determine the attitudes of your people*, Charles affirms.

*The people needed an outlet. They needed a way to come*

*together and express their grief in a public way. If we didn't organ-
ize it there would be public expressions to surface in other ways. I
knew we had to do something and guide our people to express their
pain responsibly.*

In a matter of hours word spread throughout the African
American community. On Friday, April 5, the black community
assembled at First Union Baptist Church, the very location from
which King addressed a beleaguered community in the wake of the
disappearance of the three civil rights activists four years earlier.
Charles notified Meridian police chief Gunn of their intent to march
the two miles from First Union into downtown Meridian.

*We didn't ask. We informed. We didn't get permission, but we
told them our plans to march to City Hall and assemble together on
the steps.*

Dressed in Sunday best, two thousand African American
Meridian citizens gathered to publicly grieve the death of their
national leader. His had been a voice to solidify the African
American need and desire. Falling in behind the black leaders of
Meridian, the mourners marched the two miles down 7th Avenue
singing freedom songs and proclaiming their resolve to carry the
torch of nonviolence yet non-acquiescence.

Charles led the march as the founder and president of the Meridian
Action Committee. He was flanked on either side by stalwarts of the
community. At his right was Reverend R.S. Porter, pastor of First
Union Baptist where they had all assembled. To his left was MAC vice
president Oliver Foster. Charles Young was among the men, and

nearby was James Bishop, the godfather of the African American community and owner of Enterprise Funeral Home. Hand in hand they marched, each unthreatened in the grasping of his neighbor, his masculinity affirmed in the solidarity of their united front.

There is great power claimed by a throng traveling together. The act of a march shares roots with a biblical people delivered from bondage in Egypt; a people miraculously spared through the mighty acts of an accompanying God who would usher them time and again through formidable scenarios. These American civil rights marches are one of the most biblical responses to injustice that a community can claim. There is a unique difference between these public expressions of solidarity and the public declarations of estrangement the African American community experienced in the Klan marches. One sought to inject fear into a community and silence a people. The other sought to bolster faith and courage in a community and reclaim for a people a voice.

God was with the marchers that day. Also with them were Meridian City Police. Many of the police force still shared loyalties to Klan activity to the chagrin of the chief who had been experiencing a quickened conscience. Chief Gunn wanted no violence in his city, either from the black marchers or toward them. Officers crept slowly alongside the mass of pedestrians in patrol cars, eyeing the throng of walkers behind short, stilted breaths.

Charles's voice beckoned the walkers to one old Negro spiritual after another, and they joined in the leader's songs with amazing solidarity, the line of singers spanning several city blocks.

*Oh freedom! Oh freedom! Oh freedom over me!*
*And before I'll be a slave I'll be buried in my grave*
*And go home to my Lord and be free.*

The pastor bellowed a new line, *"No more moaning!"* and the marchers followed his lead.

*No more moaning, no more moaning, no more moaning over me!*
*And before I'll be a slave I'll be buried in my grave*
*And go home to my Lord and be free.*

*"There'll be singing!"*

*There'll be singing! There'll be singing! There'll be singing over me!*
*And before I'll be a slave I'll be buried in my grave*
*And go home to my Lord and be free.*

*"There'll be shouting! ... There'll be praying! ..."*

With each verse and step the sharing of purpose and mission deepened in the massive, moving congregation. When one song ended, the cadence of marching feet was quickly accompanied by a new chant, the rhythm of the synchronized step giving structure to the message of the song...

*Ain't gonna let **nobody** turn me 'roun'*
*Turn me 'roun' ... Turn me 'roun'*
*Ain't gonna let nobody turn me 'roun'*

*I'm gonna keep on awalkin', keep on atalkin', marchin' up to freedom land*

*Ain't gonna let **no jailhouse** turn me 'roun'...*
*Turn me 'roun'... Turn me 'roun'*
*Ain't gonna let no jailhouse turn me 'roun'*
*I'm gonna keep on awalkin', keep on atalkin', marchin' up to freedom land*

*Ain't gonna let **segregation** turn me 'roun'...*
*Turn me 'roun'... Turn me 'roun'*
*Ain't gonna let segregation turn me 'roun'*
*I'm gonna keep on awalkin', keep on atalkin', marchin' up to freedom land*

*Ain't gonna let **Mississippi** turn me 'roun'*
*Turn me 'roun'... Turn me 'roun'*
*Ain't gonna let Mississippi turn me 'roun'*
*I'm gonna keep on awalkin', keep on atalkin', marchin' up to freedom land*

As the marchers neared City Hall the officers arranged themselves strategically on the perimeter of the crowd. An irony of the march destination is that the police station was located in the basement of the municipal building. Someone at City Hall had the wherewithal to lower the American flag to half mast out front. The marchers would have seen the lowered flag as they rounded the corner to gather before the steps from which the African American leaders addressed the crowd.

Like the federal structure a couple of blocks away, this building was a monument to the Golden Age of Meridian. Its broad steps rose high above the city street. Before it showered a tall and elaborate fountain spewing a vast spray of water fifteen feet into the air. While the city officials may have permitted the march and provided security, they inhibited the assembly by refusing to turn off the fountain. Throughout his address Charles hollered over the noise of the falling water, and those at the base of the stairs received a shower every time the wind blew.

From the top of the steps Charles addressed the congregation. A line of policemen bordered the crowd, armed with hard hats and billy clubs. Several white spectators congregated from a "safe" distance across the street. The marchers looked as though they had just left a Sunday meeting, dressed in dark suits and in dresses. White spectators in work clothes leaned idly against parking meters across the street. Housewives donning head scarves stopped in the middle of their Friday errands to watch the happening.

The sky was overcast and the American flag hung limply about its pole, heavy in the humid Mississippi spring.

*It is a very dismal day*...began the Meridian Action Committee president. *We are here today....*

Charles spoke slowly, summoning the authority of the African American homiletic in the open-air assembly.

*We are here today because of the death of our leader, Martin Luther King, Jr.*

The usual banter between church and preacher was noticeably absent. The crowd stood silent and attentive, straining to hear the reverend above the showering fountain.

At the perimeter of the assembly a large police officer paced impatiently in the street. He had been uneasy throughout the march and once at City Hall his eyes darted anxiously between the gathering of black mourners and the police chief who watched carefully another thirty yards away. The number of collected African Americans was a frightening sight for a man who could not imagine the redemptive qualities of black initiative.

Racism breeds a failure to trust. Officer Lee Roberts did not trust this crowd of African Americans at all, and he had little tolerance for the small, black preacher addressing the congregation from the steps of his City Hall. He hadn't liked Reverend Johnson when he met him on the steps of the federal building seven years earlier, and he didn't like Reverend Johnson this day as he summoned two thousand African American residents with an authority that the law enforcement of Meridian could not claim. This would be this officer's last day on the police force. The very next day Lee Roberts quit the Meridian Police Department.

After echoing a few lines from Dr. King's "I Have a Dream ..." speech, Charles broke into his own cadence. The crowd soon found its voice in response to his exhortation.

*We've come this far and we ain't going back!*

The crowd responded in orchestrated fashion like an organ during Sunday preaching and soon began to chant his tag line with him between verses.

*They might kill the man but they can't kill the dream!*
All together the crowd affirmed,
**"We've come this far and we ain't going back!"**

*Violence is not the answer! Why destroy the city you've helped to build?!*
**"We've come this far and we ain't going back!"**

Near the end of his message, the Meridian leader broke into song, bellowing out Dr. King's favorite hymn,

*Precious Lord, take my hand, lead me on, help me stand,*
*I am tired, I am weak, I am worn;*
*Through the storm, through the night, lead me on to the light:*
*Take my hand, precious Lord, lead me home.*

The moments marching and assembling on the steps of City Hall were a deeply religious experience for each individual in the black community. There were few places a crowd of African Americans could gather in public and not be harassed or scrutinized. This was not a private meeting held secretively in the backroom of a funeral home in the black community. They were not confining their emotions to the black business district of town, or weeping quietly in one another's living rooms. This was a public tragedy and deserved a public address. It was the proclamation of a people that communicated to a city struggling to come to terms with the age, "We are here. We have been hurt ... *again*! We have been wounded in the senseless murder of our leader, Martin Luther King, Jr. Yet, we are committed to being the kind of citizens that seek a better day, a more righteous way. Advances have been made. Greater ones must come."

Not a single incident of violence occurred that day in connection with the march. It was a peaceable demonstration of grief and a fortifying declaration of hope. The moment is a pivotal benchmark in the city's public sentiments concerning race. Meridian can thank a caring pastor from a small, holiness movement for leading a gracious response to yet another national tragedy.

# CHAPTER 17

## ALTON'S PENANCE

*The civil rights movement, unlike many colonial revolutions, does not seek to expel the oppressor: it must attempt to transform him, while it isolates the unregenerate terrorist.*
~Martin Luther King, Jr.

*O*n a warm summer day in 1977, the pastor-father stepped out of the front door of 1625 29th Avenue where his baby girl was playing on the front porch. She meandered about the elevated slab, a precipice above the sloping lawn that arched toward the street curb. The front door opened east, giving the dad an easy view south, down the street. Watching his baby girl's imagination come to life, Charles stood between her and the step that dropped to the lawn. Toys in hand she canvassed the area from the bars of one railing to the other.

Shirley, Charles's recently wed wife, was inside the house at the time. As Charles watched his daughter play he couldn't help but thank God for the woman in his life. They met, fell in love fast, and married quickly. Shirley threw herself into the ministry of Fitkin's Memorial Church and supported Charles in his many pursuits and passions. They complemented one another well during what seemed to be less hostile years of Charles's ministry, praying together, visiting together, singing together. When Charles preached Shirley chided him, "Come on, now!" And when he sang she hummed. As certainly as Charles knew how to pastor, Shirley knew how to make him a better one. Charles was very aware of these blessings.

Charles was contemplating these things, enjoying his little girl's freedom when something caught his eye. Down the hill a white man made his way up the incline of 29th Avenue. The figure made his way slowly but deliberately and looked vaguely familiar to Charles. He climbed as though he carried a heavy load.

*Is that Alton Wayne?*

Up the street trudged the white man clad in a blue jeans shirt and dark pants. He held something in both hands.

*That is Alton!*

It was Alton Wayne Roberts. Roberts had just served his sentence at the penitentiary in Leavenworth, Kansas, and returned to Mississippi to resume life in Meridian that very week. Other than TV appearances or newspaper photos, Charles had not seen Roberts since the day they sat opposite each other in the courtroom.

*Is he comin' to finish off his job? Is he comin' for me?*

A flash of fear shot through Charles's body at the sight of Alton's face. He looked back and forth between his daughter playing on the porch and the man he had testified against in federal court now ascending the street. The community was quiet. There was no activity up or down the street and Charles wished there was.

The man slowed to a stop before Charles's house at the foot of the sloping lawn where the grass and the concrete meet. He peered up to where Charles stood over his young daughter.

"Reverend Johnson, can I talk to you?" Roberts had a large object under one arm.

"Okay," the reverend answered slowly, sizing up the situation in his mind. He stepped off the porch and scaled a few steps down to the sidewalk. The ex-convict walked up a few steps from the road and they met halfway between the street and Charles's home. The two men stood toe to toe, and by now Charles could tell that Alton was visibly upset.

"Reverend Johnson, I don't know what to say," stammered the visitor, eyes red and wet. "I was young and all mixed-up. I didn't know what I was doing," he sniffed.

Charles eyed Alton carefully as the man held out a large canvas from under his arm. "I painted this picture for you in prison." He presented an amateur version of a large snowcapped mountain. "I'd like you to have it." It was a peaceful scene, the majestic peak reflected in the stillness of a serene lake at its base. In the bottom right-hand corner the name "W. Roberts" had been thinly and delicately brushed over a small knoll.

With his other hand Alton held up a string of fresh fish he'd caught just before coming to see Charles. "And I want you to have these." He lifted his hand and the twine was wrapped several times around his fingers leaving deep imprints in his skin. The weight of the fish rocked a slow pendulum back and forth, swinging the seconds into hours and the years into a moment.

"Please forgive me." Alton's eyes lifted to meet Charles's.

Charles glanced up to the porch where his baby girl moved around in the freedom of her innocence. She did not know to watch this curious interchange. She did not know to fear or even to be furious. Two men talked on the sidewalk. One of them was her Daddy.

Charles looked back at Alton. For a long time this man had been a caricature of racism, the epitome of hate. In his reckless abandon Alton was a figure to fear. Here on the street he was a shadow to be pitied. Roberts seemed sickly and frail, a stark contrast to the hulking figure with which he used to intimidate anyone in his path. Charles once saw in him the personification of bigotry, but in these moments he saw the humanity of a tortured individual.

Meanwhile a lone fish retained some fight among the cluster of ten or so others. They were so fresh they were still wet. The struggling fish arched violently curling a tail fin upward in one last hopeful gasp.

Charles reached out to accept the meager expressions of penance. He looked the man in the eyes. "I forgive you, Alton."

The trembling Roberts broke with greater emotion. Wrapping his arms around the black man in the middle of the African American neighborhood, Alton clutched Charles's back, weeping uncontrollably. Charles wept too. The two stood there for a long moment, wrapped in painful embrace, thoughts barraged by images; a federal courtroom, a dirt road, a sunken station wagon, and three tattered bodies exhumed from the raw Mississippi mud.

It is the unseen image of the civil rights fight. It is the front-page photo that *Time* magazine never ran. Imagine the headline: "Victory OR Sham?! Racist murderer walks streets a free man."

Charles knows that Alton got off light. He knows that mothers mourn their sons. A wife grieves her husband. A community demands justice. A nation is embarrassed and angry.

But for a moment the Meridian face of white supremacy and the Meridian face of black activism reconciled on 29th Avenue.

*You say, "Forgive him?! I'd throw him . . . !" Well, yes, I forgave him because that is what Christ told us to do! We forgive our enemies. No one said it would be easy. But if we love our Lord that is what we are going to do.*

*And so he gave me those things and after we hugged he turned around and just walked on down the road. I'd see him from a distance around town now and then but we never did talk after that. He died a few years ago.*

*I believe he meant it. I choose to believe he meant what he said, that he was truly sorry for what he'd done.*

Alton would live out his days a sickly remnant of the virile young man he once was. After his conviction Roberts aided the FBI as an informant of other Klan activity, and he became widely regarded as a snitch in and out of prison. Eventually he started another night club in Meridian. Had his expressions of penance and the forgiveness of Reverend Johnson served to mollify his tormented heart? Had he reached out to others to express his regret? We do not know the inner workings of a man's heart, nor the gift of peace the Almighty grants him there. But we do know that when Alton Wayne Roberts died September 11, 1999, he had been forgiven by at least one man.

As each anniversary of June 21, 1964, draws near, Charles Johnson's interpretation of the three slain activists' sacrifice is the one that shapes a forward moving Meridian and Philadelphia. "In this state, hatred flowed like a river. Where hatred rolled, freedom and love now flow," he once told a reporter. "These three men shed their blood in the state of Mississippi and because of them we have the Voting Rights Act. Because of them we have more elected Black officials in Mississippi than in any other state...We have to get to the young people and let them know what Chaney, Schwerner and Goodman did for them."[1]

We also must let others know the story of a man who wanted nothing more than to minister in obedience to God's call, who marched straight into his greatest fears, who served unwaveringly amidst adversity, who offered love to the forgotten and a voice for the acquiesced, all with the single aspiration: to help the whole man.

*If I was going to help his soul, his heart, then I was going to have to work to better his whole life.*

Charles Johnson did not intend to be a community activist. He did not set out to stand down unjust systems, or get tangled up in a national civil rights case. His passion flowed from a center more fiery than the furnace of racism. He knew that in order to be called *to* the fire one must first be called *by* the Fire

EPILOG

## REDEEMED RELATIONSHIP

*Today, finally, all America continually hears the "firebell in the night." The content of the nation's character is being determined in the contemporary tumultuous struggles.*
~Martin Luther King, Jr., 1965

or many who were involved in the civil rights fight, the period following the intense struggle was often difficult to cope with. The experience for activists in this post-activism season has been likened to the traumatic stress disorder experienced by a soldier. The distress of the conflict was so severe, so intense during the sixties that when normal life and routine was introduced again a person struggled to know how to operate. Like a soldier coming home from war, many civil rights activists wrestled with how to acclimate to society after the turbulent sixties.[1]

Charles remained highly active in civic life well beyond the 1960s. In 1971 he established Meridian's Opportunities Industrial Center (OIC). With the help of federal grant money, Charles set up a training center for young people seeking employment. He obtained a cash register and recruited some seasoned professionals to come to Fitkin's Church and teach young people how to handle money, work a cash register, or write a resumé. Civil rights concerns did not leave Charles, but he recalibrated his focus as his perception of society's most urgent needs changed.

A pivotal moment in this reordering of Charles's priorities came in 1972 after a local prayer breakfast was held for ministers in

Meridian. The special speaker for the breakfast was the Reverend Billy Graham, who was in the prime of his global crusading ministry. Charles was deeply moved by the evangelistic fervor of this minister of the gospel and sensed a conviction within his heart. After praying about the leanings of his spirit, he called the local newspaper to announce his resignation as president of the Meridian Action Committee. Charles was surprised when not only did the newspaper come to report his story, but the local TV station also showed up with cameras.

"I must be about my Father's business," Charles offered as he described his reordering of priorities. Some may think he had just now found religion, the activist explained. It wasn't that he didn't have it before, he just had a deep conviction that this was the direction where God wanted him to focus his energies. He set about planning a crusade in Meridian at a local high school stadium. It was a time of renewal in the life of the preacher as he invested himself in evangelistic concerns that were somewhat stolen from him as a new preacher in Mississippi in 1961.

Charles focused on relationships and opportunity to spread the gospel. At one point his church rented out an old juke joint in the historic black business district around the corner from Young's Hotel. They wired the storefront with speakers outside and played Christian music loudly down the street on the weekends. A large cross was posted in the plate glass window, lit up with light bulbs running up and down and side to side. Church members went to the little urban mission and planted themselves on the sidewalks to mingle with the Saturday night crowd seeking a weekend party. When they could lure some visitors through the door Charles was ready to preach with the Word in his hand and a pulpit at his feet. He delivered an evangelistic sermon and invited people to know Jesus.

*I actually got a few members out of that deal! We cleaned that section of town up, too. People stopped going down there so much. They heard the music and wanted to dance but then felt guilty because it was music about God. We really messed with them!*

While Charles burned with evangelistic fervor, an integrated church began to express interest in Charles's leadership. Talmadge Johnson was the Mississippi district superintendent who cemented Charles's role in the integrated district in 1975. The two forged a powerful bond of fellowship that enabled others in the broader church to trust the Meridian pastor. He also advocated for Charles outside of Mississippi. He connected Charles with the directors of the General Assembly and arranged for the Fitkin's Memorial Choir to sing at the 1976 Assembly in Dallas, Texas. Then in 1978 Charles and Shirley were invited to sing at an evangelism conference in Oklahoma City.

*We sang "The Blood Will Never Lose Its Power" and the place just lit up. It really came alive!*

Events like these really put the Johnsons and the Fitkin's church on the map. Soon, the denominational magazine called the *Herald of Holiness* featured an article on Fitkin's Memorial Church called, "Black Nazarene Church Emerging as Evangelistic Force." Charles was being invited all over the country to hold revival services or to speak at camp meetings. Suddenly, a man with whom the greater church did not know how to relate ten years earlier was being celebrated for his spirited fervor and commitment to the holiness message.

This was also a period in which the Mississippi legislature sought to make amends with key black leaders of the state. Mississippi governor William Waller appointed Charles to the Governor's Commission on Civil Rights. While serving on this commission, Charles served alongside a certain judge from Meridian named Lee Roberts. Lee had become a justice of the peace since those early days on the police force. From time to time he'd beckon Charles with a smile, "When we gonna get that cup of coffee together?" It was a little hard for the preacher to swallow, considering how hateful and violent the man had acted toward him before. Charles had a hard time trusting it was genuine. They never have had that cup of coffee.

Governor Cliff Finch worked to "lift up" the African American leaders around the state. He appointed Charles a Colonel on his governor's staff and adopted the pastor in his "Lunchbox Club," an honor that granted Charles access to the governor's mansion at any time of the day.

During Finch's tenure as governor, Charles and Shirley Johnson attended a private banquet at the governor's mansion where there was an elaborate door prize of a brand new Cadillac. Charles teased the staff on his way out of the door that night:

*Now, when y'all pull my number just give me a call at home and I'll come back for my Cadillac. So you just call me.*

When the Johnsons walked in the door of their Meridian home that night, Charles thought it was a joke from the governor's staff when the phone rang and he heard: "You won the Cadillac! Come back and get it."

*But, that's what we did. We drove right back over to Jackson that night and got our new Cadillac.*

Another politician who recognized the contributions Charles had made to civic life was an unlikely presidential candidate from a peanut farm in Georgia. Jimmy Carter personally sought Charles's support in his campaign. Charles was not overly impressed by the farmer and, besides, he had already pledged his support to former vice president Hubert Humphrey.

*"I'm sorry, Mr. Carter. I'm a Humphrey man," he told the candidate.*

Charles was surprised and embarrassed when Carter took the 1976 Democratic primaries. What Charles did not know was that Hubert Humphrey had already been diagnosed with cancer and, despite encouragement from supporters, had decided not to run for president. President Carter did not hold it against Charles, however, and ended up appointing the Meridian pastor to his Manpower Board for economic development in Mississippi. When President Carter invited the Johnsons to his inaugural ball, Charles declined on moral grounds:

*I didn't go because I knew they'd have all that bubbly stuff there.*

Local leaders eventually came to recognize the value in Charles's social activism. Mike Watkins, Lauderdale County lawyer and member of the defense who referred to civil rights activists as "low-class riff-raff" in his closing argument, eventually congratulated Charles for his integrity and perseverance in the struggle. He later told Shirley Johnson, "I really do appreciate what your husband has done for his people in the community," and asked for Charles's verbal support of a new community center in Philadelphia.

By 1984 Charles was appointed Coordinator for Black Nazarene Ministries by the General Church of the Nazarene. He knew whom to honor at the very first Black Churchman's Conference held in Orlando, Florida. It was a humble man who never asked for much, never complained at all, and always served to encourage others in the call to serve Christ: Charles's former superintendent of the Gulf Central District, Warren Rogers.

Warren had sent the young Charles to a place the preacher was terrified to go: Fitkin's Memorial[2] Church of the Nazarene. It seemed such an insignificant location in a highly volatile situation. How could the work be worth the risk? It seemed undesirable and unreliable for future growth. The odds were stacked against it and against the preacher who went there. Warren Rogers had seen something in the young preacher. He had believed in Charles, and furthermore, trusted in the God Who sent him to Mississippi.

One of the great distinctions of Charles's career was receiving a doctor of divinity degree from Trevecca Nazarene College[3] in Nashville, Tennessee. This was the denominational school that

Charles could not attend when he sought ministerial training as a young man. In 1986, twenty-seven years after he set out for Bible College, Trevecca asked Charles to come to Nashville so that they could confer upon him an honorary doctorate.

When Charles went to Nashville to receive the degree, he was proud to have a very important man in his life standing right beside him. C.R. Smith was there to support the young man he sent to Bible College so many years earlier. It seemed so very appropriate that the two would converge on this property, a symbol of the journey a single man has made, a church has made, a nation has made.

It is always more beautiful to look back at what God has done than to try and make sense of it before it happens. This must be why obedience is such a virtue in the journey with God. The Word simply comes and we are given an opportunity to live in regard for God's directions or to abandon them for more popular alternatives. When one asks Charles Johnson how he feels about Mississippi, now, his answer is always the same: "It will take as much to get me to leave Mississippi as it took to get me here. I love this place. I love Mississippi!"

Dr. Charles Johnson has lived in humble obedience to the Word of God. As far as he could discern, the plan of God was not an elaborate one. It was actually quite simple and started with a familiar biblical mandate: "Go."

And so he did.

# NOTES

## Introduction

1. Walter Wink, *The Powers That Be* (Three Rivers Press, reprint, 1999), 32.

## Chapter 1

1. Booker T. Washington, 1895 Atlanta Compromise Speech (http://histo rymatters.gmu.edu/d/39/) (accessed 10/13/12).

2. Jack Nelson's description of Charles Johnson in *Terror in the Night* (Simon & Schuster, 1993), 108.

3. In those three years indictments were thrown out three times before the Supreme Court reinstated them. By that time the case listed eighteen defendants.

4. James 5:12: "Above all, my beloved, do not swear, either by heaven or by earth or by any other oath, but let your 'Yes' be yes and your 'No' be no, so that you may not fall under condemnation" (NRSV).

5. Florence Mars, *Witness in Philadelphia* (Louisiana State University Press, 1977), 229.

6. The courtroom proceedings are on public record at the Southeast Branch of the National Archives in Atlanta, Georgia. The author is greatly indebted to the research work of Douglas Linder, Professor of Law at University of Missouri Kansas City. His website on the 1967 MIBURN trial is an excellent resource for further study on the case: http://law2.umkc.edu/faculty/projects/ftrials/price&bowers/price&bowers.htm

7. *Witness in Philadelphia,* 235

## Chapter 2

1. Anthony Walton, *Mississippi: An American Journey* (Vintage, 1997), 163-164.

## Chapter 3

1. John Perkins, *He's My Brother* (Chosen Books, 1994), 27.

2. www.drphillips.org (accessed 10/13/12).

3. "Phillips Improved Pasteurization Made Orange Juice Taste Better," Mark Andrews (*Orlando Sentinel,* December 19, 1993).

4. www.drphillips.org (accessed 10/13/12).

5. The center was named after the first Black recreational superintendent, John H. Jackson, in 1995 after a major remodeling project.

6. It's been said that the origin of "love" for zero points in tennis is from the expression, "playing for love," which means to play for mere enjoyment.

## Chapter 4

1. Booker T. Washington (http://www.brainyquote.com/quotes/quotes/
b/bookertwa139251.html) (accessed 10/13/12).
2. Mark Schlueb, "Charity Founder C.R. Smith dies at 77," (*Orlando
Sentinel,* Saturday, December 20, 2003), B2.

## Chapter 5

1. *Mississippi: An American Journey,* 140.
2. More than one Nazarene Bible College grad from West Virginia has
emphasized the impact of the primary theological text on his or her life;
see *Foundations of Doctrine in Scripture and Experience,* by Harry E.
Jessop (first published in 1938).

## Chapter 7

1. Robert Kennedy, from remarks he made to the Cleveland City Club,
Cleveland, Ohio, April 5, 1968. (http://www.jfklibrary.org/Research/
Ready-Reference/RFK-Speeches/Remarks-of-Senator-Robert-F-Kennedy-
to-the-Cleveland-City-Club-Cleveland-Ohio-April-5-1968.aspx) (accessed
10/13/12).
2. "Freedom Riders," *American Experience* (PBS documentary; May,
2011).
3. Ibid.

## Chapter 8

1. Isaiah 54:17, KJV.

## Chapter 9

1. Zora Neale Hurston, "Negro Religious Customs—The Sanctified
Church" (Stetson Kennedy Archive, RG 158, S 1583, Box 1 FF 4, FSA).

## Chapter 10

1. http://www.apush-xl.com/Missburning.html (accessed 10/13/12).
2. *Terror in the Night,* 28.
3. Ibid., 113.
4. Ibid., 28.
5. William Bradford Huie, *Three Lives for Mississippi* (University Press of Mississippi, 2000), 54-55.

## Chapter 11

1. Douglas O. Linder, "Bending Toward Justice; John Doar and the Mississippi Burning Trial" essay published in *Mississippi Law Journal* (Volume 72, No. 2, Winter 2002) (http://law2.umkc.edu/faculty/projects/ftrials/trialheroes/doaressay.html) (accessed 10/13/12).
2. *Terror in the Night,* 108.
3. Gunn did not become police chief in Meridian until 1965.
4. http://www.nobelprize.org/nobel_prizes/peace/laureates/1964/king-acceptance.html (accessed 10/13/12).
5. "Bending Toward Justice."
6. See Chapter 1, note 3.
7. "Bending Toward Justice."
8. *Witness in Philadelphia,* 207-210.
9. "Bending Toward Justice."

## Chapter 12

1. Walter Wink, *The Powers That Be* (Three Rivers Press, reprint, 1999), 31.
2. *Terror in the Night,* 108.
3. Ibid., 109.

## Chapter 13

1. http://law2.umkc.edu/faculty/projects/ftrials/price&bowers/klan.htm (accessed 10/13/12).

2. Quotations from the trial transcript, http://law2.umkc.edu/faculty/projects/ftrials/price&bowers/Johnson.html (accessed 10/13/12).

3. *Witness in Philadelphia,* 235.

## Chapter 14

1. Elie Wiesel's response at the Honors College Convocation (February 8, 2010) for the University of Mississippi in response to a question from the audience: "How do you respond to the antagonists who claim the memory of the Holocaust will die when your generation dies?"

2. This was the FBI's title for this case, usually abbreviated to the acronym "MIBURN trial."

3. *Terror in the Night,* 112-113.

4. Seth Cagin and Philip Dray, *We Are Not Afraid* (Macmillan, 1988), 14.

5. The word "Negro" next to Schwerner's and Goodman's names was later scratched out and replaced with "White."

6. Cagin and Dray, 27.

## Chapter 15

1. *Witness in Philadelphia,* 256.

2. Ibid., 257.

3. Ibid., 257-258.

4. Ibid., 258.

5. The jury had only deliberated for nine of those twenty-four hours.

6. Killen was later convicted for the crime of these three murders in 2005 and currently serves three consecutive twenty-year sentences.

7. *Witness in Philadelphia,* 262.

## Chapter 16

1. http://www.jfklibrary.org/Research/Ready-Reference/RFK-Speeches/Statement-on-the-Assassination-of-Martin-Luther-King.aspx (accessed 10/13/12).

## Chapter 17

1. Les Bayless, *People's Weekly World* (25 May, 1996), cited on Spartacus Educational website: <http://www.spartacus.schoolnet.co.uk/USAchaney.htm> (accessed 10/13/12).

## Epilog

1. Thanks to Dr. Marvin King, assistant professor of political science at the University of Mississippi, for helping me understand this social dynamic.

2. Obviously, a church with the word "Memorial" in its name is going to have a story. In the small country of Swaziland located at the southern tip of the dark continent called Africa is a hospital that shares a unique name with the Mississippi church. It is the Raleigh Fitkin Memorial Hospital established by a grieving mother who wanted the legacy of her deceased son to continue. "RFM, as it is locally known...has 350 beds with an occupancy rate of 65-70% per month. Around 400 clients visit the outpatient department on a daily basis. It provides medical, surgical, pediatrics, obstetrics, emergency and rehabilitative services." With a heart for African ministry, Mrs. Fitkin also expressed a deep concern that African Americans not be forgotten in the church's attention to missions. In the name of her son, the grieving mother funded the establishment of the humble Fitkin's Memorial Church of the Nazarene in Meridian, Mississippi. It was there that the denomination held its "First Negro Conference in the South of the Church of the Nazarene" in 1948. And from this location General Superintendent John Knight expressed a growing

desire to reach African Americans in the state of Florida as well. It is very possible that the growing evangelical concern for Florida Nazarenes that led to Charles's salvation in the 1950s was born in the very location to which he was sent to serve for more than fifty years of ministry. (http://swazivolunteers.com/Volunteer_programmes/Raleigh_fitkin_mem orial_hospital_medical_nursing_volunteering_swaziland.asp) (Wesley L. Bishop, *Charles Johnson, The Church of the Nazarene, and Civil Rights in Meridian, Mississippi; a Thesis in Candidacy for the Degree Master of Arts.* East Carolina University. Greenville, North Carolina: April, 2011)

3. Currently Trevecca Nazarene University.